£1.2...

SATAN

The Prince
Of
Darkness

SATAN

The Prince Of Darkness

By
FREDK. A. TATFORD, Litt.D.

KREGEL PUBLICATIONS
Grand Rapids, Michigan 49501

SATAN, The Prince of Darkness by Fredk. A. Tatford originally published by Prophetic Witness Publishing House, Eastbourne, Sussex, England under title, *The Prince of Darkness*. All rights reserved. This edition published under special arrangements with originating publisher.

Library of Congress Catalog Card Number 74-82808

ISBN 0-8254-3807-1

Printed in the United States of America

CONTENTS

PREFACE

WHEN, in a past age, the highest of the angelic hierarchy inspired an audacious rebellion against the Creator, there commenced an age-long conflict, which still continues to the present day. The Bible discloses little of the events which led to the loss by these mighty spirits of their pristine innocence and holiness, but it is clear that their revolt was deliberate and determined, and their fall was therefore inevitable.

Whatever retribution may have been suffered at the time, final judgment has been delayed, but the attitude of the rebels remains unchanged. Their great leader, Lucifer (the shining one), has become Satan (the adversary) and is still the inspiration of their opposition to the Eternal. The rebellion continues and, for centuries past, has been evidenced particularly in the attempts to thwart the Divine purposes of blessing for man and to arouse the human race to active enmity to God.

The Scriptures tell something of the history of "the prince of darkness" and of his struggle against the Almighty, and they reveal the ultimate victory of God over Satan and good over evil. The following pages are an attempt to summarise the Biblical teaching on an enthralling and extremely important subject.

FREDK. A. TATFORD

CHAPTER I

PRINCIPLE OR PERSON

THE origin of sin is a problem which has perplexed philo-
sopher and thinker from the earliest days of history
and to which, in consequence, many a solution has been
propounded. Existentialism, for example, suggests that sin
originated in man's endeavour to find security " outside the
tension of the didactical relation between time and eternity."
Marxism, on the other hand, implies that sin sprang from
unbalanced social relationships and can be eliminated only
by a victorious conclusion to the class war. Neo-orthodoxy
maintains that sin resulted from man's refusal to remain
within his appointed limits. There is, of course, a modicum
of truth in all of these suggestions, but none provides a
satisfactory solution.

The primitive savage instinctively feels that his surround-
ings are evil rather than good and, personifying his fears,
as Tulloch says, " he trembles before a power or powers
which can hurt him, blight the fruits of his labour or
destroy his cattle, deny his success in the chase, or triumph
in war; and he offers rites or uses spells or incantations to
drive away those powers, or draw them to his side. The
evil is therefore truly far more of a god to him than the
good, and devil-worship . . . is only a natural inference of
the savage view of life and of nature." Evil is obviously
present in nature, but is it identifiable with nature or is it
the work of some invisible power such as that conjectured
by the savage?

It was originally contended that evil has always existed
and that it is an essential counterpart of good. If evil is
eternal and absolute, however, there is a limitation on the
omnipotence and holiness of God. It was subsequently
argued by early gnostics that all evil was identifiable with
matter; that, in fact, matter was inherently evil and antagonistic to God. Matter, being, in their view, eternal, was
not created by God — again a derogation from His power
— and He fashioned the universe out of matter already
existing. " Man is a microcosm; the enemy of the highest
principle within him is the material sensuous element,
which is not merely the occasion or instrument of sin, but

in itself is intrinsically evil." Prof. G. A. Knight says in *A Biblical Approach to the Doctrine of the Trinity*, " While evil comes from the free choice of the free will of man, it also seems inherent in the universe outside man." It is true that sin is universal, but the implication that it is attached to the material world is obviously fallacious. Human depravity may be universal, but matter is not *per se* sinful.

The Syrian gnostics went farther and, to quote Neander, " assumed the existence of an active, turbulent kingdom of evil, or of darkness, which, by its encroachment on the kingdom of light, brought about a commixture of the light with the darkness."

In some respects, a closer approximation to the truth is found in Persian dualism. The Persians conceived of the world as divided into two realms, one of which was good and the other evil, and each of which was reigned over by an independent deity. The ruler of the evil realm was considered to be responsible for the introduction of sin into the world. The ruler of the good realm, it was taught, would ultimately vanquish the god of the evil realm and cleanse the world of that which defiles it. The evil ruler was sometimes said to have the power (equally with the good ruler) to create, and by his work, creatures were brought into existence who were opposed to the Divine will. These two coeval and co-eternal powers of good and evil were constantly struggling for the government of the universe. In Iranian dualism, the supreme God was Anra Mazda or Spenta Mainyu, and opposed to him was the evil one, Anra Mainyu. In later Persian literature, these two opposing spirits became Ormuzd and Ahriman. In Egypt, the same rival principles found expression in Osiris (the good spirit) and Typhon (the evil spirit).

In later thought, the creation of both spirits was said to have been the work of the Supreme God. Lactantius, for example, taught that, " before the creation of the world, God produced a spirit (the Logos) like Himself, and that He then made another being, in whom the disposition of the Divine origin did not remain. This being, of his own volition, became infected with evil, and consequently acquired for himself another name. He is called by the Greeks *diabolos*, but we call him *criminator*, because he reports to God the faults to which he entices us."

" In the third century," as Tulloch writes, " dualism took fresh life and burst forth with new momentum under the name of Manicheeism. This system especially emphasised the power of evil as a distinct and co-eternal principle in antagonism to the good. . . . It sprang up again suddenly in the East in the twelfth century, founding a new sect under the name of Paulicians." But we must leave those interested in the subject to pursue it in Neander's *General History of the Christian Religion and Church.*

During the captivity, the Israelites were brought into contact with the teaching of the Persian Zoroastrianism and many commentators have suggested that it was from thence that the Jewish doctrine of a personal devil derived its origin. This is manifestly incorrect, for the Scriptures had referred to the existence of this mighty being at a much earlier date. It should, however, be said that it is not universally accepted unfortunately that the Biblical references are to a person rather than to a principle and the alternative view has been put quite incisively by Dr. Horace Bushnell, " There is no more reason to suppose that God created any such being or that any such being really exists, than there is to suppose that there is a real being called the prince of this world, or another called antichrist, or two others called God and Magog. The devil is that objective person, whose reality is the sum of all subjective seductions, or temptations to evil, *viz.,* those of bad spirits, and those of the corrupted soul itself. These bad spirits sometimes called Legion, together with our own bad thoughts, are all gathered up into a great king of art and mischief, and called the devil. Whether it is done by some instinct of language, or some special guidance of inspiration in the use of language or both, we do not know : the latter is more probable. But however it comes to pass, we can see that it serves a most important use in the economy of revelation. In the process of recovery to God, men must be convinced of their sins, and made thoroughly conscious of their guiltiness, and this requires a turning of their minds upon themselves in reflection, and a state of piercingly subjective attention to their own ill-desert. And yet they must be taken away, somehow, from a too close or totally subjective attention even to their sins. For if they are to be taken away from their ill-desert or guiltiness, they must be drawn out into a movement of soul in exactly the opposite direction, *viz.,* in the direction of faith which is outward. And this is exactly what the grand objective conception of the devil prepares and facilitates. First, their sin is all gathered up, with its roots and causes, into the bad king conceived to be reigning without; and then it is permitted the penitent, or the disciple struggling with his enemy, to conceive that Christ, in whom he is called to believe, is out in force, to subdue and crush the monster." We have quoted *in extenso* because the same kind of teaching is still prevalent, but, so far from it being possible to believe that Satan is an objective conception, experience itself witnesses that there is a vital and powerful influence constantly exerting itself against all who would walk worthily of God.

In the world generally, there is rarely belief in the personality of the evil one. The devil of theology is often referred to in ridicule as some dark monstrosity with frightening physical characteristics of horns, hoofs and tail, and armed with a pitchfork. It is more commonly maintained, however, that " he is an abstract principle of evil — that absence of good, a negation. The words which Goethe put into the mouth of Mephistopheles in *Faust*, ' I am the spirit of negation,' are the popular definition of the devil today. He is impersonal, immaterial, impossible."

Yet there must patently be an evil personality behind the happenings in this world. " Some think," writes Summers, " that evil is merely a blind, vagrant, undetermined force, not regulated, irresponsible, wandering and random energy. Surely it must be apparent to the shallowest mind that the evil of the world is too masterly marshalled, too subtly planned, too skilfully directed, too logically remorseless, for any such facile explanation. There is design; there is diplomacy; there is cunning; there are stratagems and campaigns. There must be a master mind behind these activities." " The devil does not exist," declared Maxim Gorki. " The devil is an invention of our evil imagination. Men have invented him to justify their sinfulness, and also in the interest of God, in order not to wrong Him." But Beaudelaire was quite right when he said, " The devil's neatest trick is to persuade us that he does not exist."

The Scriptures clearly teach, not the unceasing conflict between two principles, nor the objective personification of evil for the purpose of drawing the soul out of itself, but the existence of a mighty spirit being who is in antagonism to

God. (See Matt. 13 : 39; John 13 : 2; Acts 5 : 3; 1 Pet. 5 : 8.)
" The personal existence of a spirit of evil," says Barry, " is
revealed again and again in Scripture. Every quality, every
action, which can indicate personality, is attributed to him
in language which cannot be explained away." He is capable of existence and intelligent movement (Job 1 : 7, 12);
he deliberately enters into men (John 13 : 27), he craftily
lays snares for them (1 Tim. 3 : 7; 2 Tim. 2 : 26), he tempted
our Lord (Matt. 4 : 1-11), he inflicts disease (Job 2 : 7) and
imprisonment (Rev. 2 : 10), he is capable of speech (Job
1 : 7-11), of anger (Rev. 12 : 12) and of deceit (Rev. 20 : 8),
he is described by Christ as a liar and a murderer (John
8 : 44), and by John as a sinner (1 John 3 : 8), and other
activities and characteristics are credited to him which can
only be applicable to a person. If the testimony of our Lord
is to be accepted — quite apart from any of the other state-
ments of the Word of God — there can be no dubiety
regarding the personality of Satan. Findlay says, " In the
visible forms of sin, Jesus saw the shadow of this great
antagonist. From the Evil One, He taught His disciples to
pray that they might be delivered. The victims of disease
and madness whom He healed were so many captives
rescued from the malignant power of Satan. And when
Jesus went to meet His death, He viewed it as the supreme
conflict with the usurper and oppressor who claimed to be
' the prince of this world '."

The revelation of the Bible is that there is a mighty ruler
of darkness, who deliberately sets himself in opposition to
God and His people; that that great being is neither eternal
nor self-existent, but a creation of God's hands; yet, nevertheless, one whose influence is far-reaching and whose power
is reasonably to be feared. His *modus operandi*, his media,
his machinations, his authority and his programme are so
clearly delineated in the pages of Holy Writ that ignorance
of them is inexcusable, but his ceaseless activity and constant scheming demand the meticulous study of the Divine
revelation of his character and ways.

As Sir Robert Anderson has pointed out in *The Silence of
God*, there is often a complete misconception of the character and activities of the devil. " The Satan of Christian
mythology," he writes, " is a monster of wickedness, the
instigator to every crime of exceptional brutality or loathsome lust." But this is really a calumny. " When a man

is led into evil courses, ' he is drawn away by his own lust ' (Jas. 1: 14). The human heart, our Lord Himself declares, is the vile spring from which immoralities and crime proceed (Mk. 7: 20-23). Using the word ' immoral ' in its narrow, popular sense, there is no basis for the belief that Satan ever provokes to an immoral act." He is far more concerned with religion than with vice or wrongdoing.

The mental picture of Satan usually held is completely inaccurate. In the Middle Ages, as Papini says, he was depicted as " a bestial, hirsute and deformed monster with eyes aflame and a leering mouth, almost always naked, equipped with high horns, a long tail, and goatlike or equine hooves, and he diffused around him a fecal or sulphureous stench." Nothing could be farther from the truth. To quote Anderson again, " Men dream of a devil, horned and hoofed — a hideous and obscene monster — who haunts the squalid slums and gilded vice-dens of our cities, and tempts the depraved to acts of atrocity or shame. But, according to Holy Writ, ' he fashions himself into an angel of light ' and ' his ministers fashion themselves as ministers of righteousness ' (2 Cor. 11: 14, 15)." Far from supporting the theory that he is repellent and unattractive, the Scriptures show that he was originally possessed of exceptional wisdom and outstanding beauty, of considerable power and of great dignity.

CHAPTER II

THE ANOINTED CHERUB

SATAN is neither self-existent nor eternal. The Scriptures make clear that he is a created being and came into existence by the hand of God and initially owed his allegiance to his Maker. Little is revealed concerning his early history, but occasional glimpses are given in the Scriptures. One of the most significant of these is in Ezek. 28: 12-19. In the earlier verses of Ezek. 28 the prophet foretold the judgment of "the prince of Tyrus", but in verse 12 he commenced "a lamentation" on "the king of Tyrus". That these were not merely different appellations of the same individual is clear from the text: what is said of the prince is appropriate to an earthly potentate, but the description given of the king is patently irrelevant to a human being.

The ruler of Tyre at the time of Ezekiel's prophecy was Ithobal II and it was doubtless to him that the message of verses 2 to 10 was addressed. Tyre was built on a rocky island and was strongly fortified. Ithobal boasted of the strength and impregnability of his sea-girt city. He was extremely successful in commerce and had acquired vast riches for himself and his people, and he attributed this to his own wisdom and foresightedness. Pride so filled his breast that he claimed equality in power and wisdom with the gods. This is exactly the picture portrayed in the prophecy and Ezekiel declared that the "terrible of the nations" (*i.e.*, the Chaldeans) should assail him and that his death should prove the falsity of his claims to deity. Not long afterwards the Chaldeans turned against Tyre, invested the city and slew its ruler. The sin of the prince of Tyre was personal pride, which led him even to claim the position of deity. It is not without significance that centuries later, the Tyrians flattered King Herod that his voice was the voice of a god and that he too, refraining from rejecting their sycophantic flattery, perished at the hand of the Almighty (Acts 12: 20-23).

The "lamentation" in Ezek. 28: 12-19, whilst addressed to an earthly ruler, obviously goes beyond the king of Tyre and applies to an even greater power, who is the unseen controller. "Thou, who sealest up the measure of perfection, full of wisdom and perfect in beauty, thou wast in Eden, the garden of God. Every precious stone was thy covering: the sardius, the topaz, and the diamond, the chrysolite, the onyx, and the jasper, the sapphire, the carbuncle, and the emerald and gold. The workmanship (possibly *service*) of thy tambours and of thy pipes was in thee: in the day that thou wast created were they prepared. Thou wast the anointed covering (or *protecting*) cherub, and I had set thee so: thou wast upon the holy mountain of God; thou didst walk up and down in the midst of the stones of fire. Thou wast perfect in thy ways from the day that thou wast created " (vv. 12-15). It is reasonably clear that these words apply to Satan. He was, therefore, brought into being by the Almighty and, in his first estate, was of the highest angelic order and stood in the closest proximity to God Himself. He was " the anointed covering cherub " and was so appointed by Divine intention. The precise nature and functions of the cherubim are not explicitly stated in Scripture, although there are several references to these glorious beings. When man was expelled from the garden of Eden, cherubim were set at the east of the garden with a revolving sword of flame to ensure that no presumptuous hand reached out to pluck of the tree of life (Gen. 3: 24). They were not there, of course, to exclude man permanently from blessing.

In his *Expository Dictionary*, W. E. Vine renders the latter part of Gen. 3: 24, " at the east of the garden of Eden, He caused to dwell in a tabernacle the cherubim, and the flaming sword which turned itself to keep the way of the tree of life " and adds, " This was not simply to keep fallen human beings out; the presence of the cherubim suggests that redeemed men, restored to God on God's conditions would have access to the tree of life — see Rev. 22: 14."

In the holy of holies of the earthly tabernacle, the golden mercy-seat, which was virtually the throne of God in the midst of His people, was overshadowed by two golden cherubim, beaten out of the ends of the mercy-seat (Exod. 25: 18-22; see also Psa. 80: 1 and Heb. 9: 5). In addition, designs of cherubim were made in the tabernacle curtains and the inner veil (Exod. 26: 1, 31). When Solomon built his magnificent temple, he constructed two large cherubim of olive wood overlaid with gold, which stood with outstretched wings in the holy of holies (1 Kings 6: 23-28), overshadowing the ark of the covenant (1 Kings 8: 7).

Moreover, the decorations carved on the walls and doors of the temple included figures of cherubim (1 Kings 6: 29, 32). Psa. 18: 10 pictures the Almighty as riding upon a cherub as He descends from heaven in judgment.

The fullest description of the cherubim is given by the prophet Ezekiel (Ezek. 1: 5-28; 10: 11-22), but there are vital differences between the mysterious beings whom he saw and those previously referred to by the same name. The cherubim of the tabernacle and the temple had each two wings and they overshadowed the mercy-seat upon which the shekinah glory rested. The cherubim of Ezekiel's visions had four faces and four wings and also a wheel, and both they and the wheels were full of eyes, and, in contrast with the mercy-seat cherubim, the throne of God was above them and not overshadowed by them. (The cherubim are not, of course, identical with the "seraphim" of Isa. 6: 2, 3, nor with the "living creatures" of Rev. 4: 6-8; the latter indeed appear to combine the features of both the cherubim and the seraphim.) The responsibilities of the cherubim seem to be associated with the governmental purposes of God and judicial vindication of His character: they are upholders of the Throne of righteousness and maintain it inviolate from any infringement of justice.

Satan then was created by God for immediate attendance upon Himself and was placed in a position of close relationship with the Throne. He was upon the holy mountain of God — obviously the place of the Almighty's presence in visible glory and possibly identical with "the mount of assembly" of Isa. 14: 13 — and he walked up and down in the midst of the stones of fire. When Moses, Aaron, Nahab, Abihu and the seventy elders of Israel were summoned to Mount Sinai to meet Jehovah, they saw under His feet a pavement, resembling a transparent sapphire, and the cloud of His glory was like a consuming fire (Exod. 24: 10, 17). Again in Ezek. 1: 13, the appearance of the cherubim was said to have been like burning coals of fire, and an expanse of terrible crystal stretched over their heads (v. 22). The Eternal is a consuming fire and His intrinsic holiness is like a flame before which only the undefiled may stand. Yet, cherished and honoured above all created intelligences, the anointed cherub walked freely in the celestial sphere and basked in the intimacy of God.

Possessing Divinely-given knowledge, obviously in excess

of that of any other living creature, he was "full of wisdom". His intellectual capacity was patently of an extraordinary degree, and his understanding and discernment were fostered by the Almighty. Surpassing all other created beings in his marvellous beauty, he is described as "perfect in beauty". None was comparable in appearance to him; his attractiveness was superlative. The phraseology used by the prophet seems hyperbolical, but it is clearly intended to be taken literally. The "anointed cherub" of that bygone day sealed up the measure of perfection: he was the noblest and most perfect part of the handiwork of God, without equal or peer.

His anointing appears to have been for a particular service, for his creation synchronised with the preparation of musical instruments for his service. Pember suggests that "he awoke to consciousness to find the air filled with the rejoicing music of those whom God had appointed to stand before him". It is possible that what is implied is that the strains of music sounded forth his royal glory, but it seems more probable that he was anointed as leader of the worship of the angelic hosts and other created beings to the One who sits as supreme Sovereign. To Him all glory belongs and that right He does not devolve to a creature.

Not only did Satan find a place on "the mountain of God", but he was also found in "Eden, the garden of God" Although he certainly was present in the Adamic Eden as an apostate and tempter, it seems fairly clear that the reference is to an earlier Eden, specially prepared for him. In it was erected a palace (or "covering") of gold and precious stones, the dazzling splendour of that glorious building revealing the Divine approval of that mighty spirit. Authority over the earth and its original inhabitants was divinely conferred upon him and he still bears the title of "prince of this world", his legitimate right to that dignity being in fact recognised by our Lord (John 14: 30). Pember considers it probable that his authority comprehended the whole of the solar system and writes, "if there be truth in the accounts given by astronomers of the ruined condition of the moon . . . it would seem likely that Satan's power extends so far. And it may be also that the catastrophe to the sun, which was remedied on the fourth day (Gen. 1: 16), testifies to his connection with that glorious luminary."

The recipient of such amazing blessing and favour as were

bestowed upon Satan might well have been expected to exhibit the utmost loyalty to his Benefactor, but an inordinate pride and overweening ambition led to his tragic fall instead (1 Tim. 3: 6). "Thou wast perfect in thy ways from the day thou wast created, till unrighteousness was found in thee. By the abundance of thy traffic they filled the midst of thee with violence, and thou hast sinned; therefore have I cast thee as profane from the mountain of God, and have destroyed thee, O covering cherub, from the midst of the stones of fire. Thy heart was lifted up because of thy beauty; thou hast corrupted thy wisdom by reason of thy brightness: I have cast thee to the ground, I have laid thee before kings, that they may behold thee. By the multitude of thine iniquities, by the unrighteousness of thy traffic, thou hast profaned thy sanctuaries: and I have brought forth a fire out of the midst of thee — it hath consumed thee; and I have brought thee to ashes upon the earth, in the sight of all them that behold thee. All they that know thee among the peoples shall be amazed at thee: thou art become a terror, and thou shalt never be any more" (Ezek. 28: 15-19).

In the wisdom of God, Satan — like the other sentient creatures of the Divine hand — was in possession, not only of intelligence, wisdom and sensibility, but also of personal free-will. In his pristine ingenuousness, his affections and loyalties were obviously directed to his Creator and the whole inclination of his being was towards the fulfilment of the Divine will. He was immaculate in character and service until that awful moment when unrighteousness was found in him. Verse 16 infers that his sin sprang from a corruption in which others had a part, but in which he personally had the primary responsibility. The word translated "traffic" might also be rendered "slanders". On later occasions the devil slandered his Maker to Eve (Gen. 3: 1-5) and slandered Job to God (Job 1: 11, etc.) and, as "the accuser of the brethren", he still carries slanderous reports to the courts of heaven regarding the actions of men. Satan's sin was pride (1 Tim. 3: 6). "He is king over all the sons of pride" (Job 41: 34). Conscious of his personal attractions, his exceptional mental endowments, his general superiority to his fellows, and the glory of his exalted position, he evidently slandered the Almighty to those subservient spirits who surrounded him and did his bidding, and their very praise and adulation filled him with even greater thoughts of violence. In astounding arrogance, he sought the supreme place in heaven. Whether he endeavoured to divert the worship of the angelic hosts from the Creator to himself, or whether he attempted to put himself on the throne of the Almighty is not explicitly revealed, but he deliberately made his choice and, despite all the benefactions of the Eternal, turned in revolt against Him.

There could be only one outcome of such a rebellion. Long afterwards, the preacher put it succinctly when he said, " Pride goeth before destruction, and a haughty spirit before a fall " (Prov. 16: 18). Satan was expelled from the highest heights and cast as a profane thing out of the mountain of God and removed for ever from the stones of fire. Isaiah gives a further glimpse of that dark hour when he writes: " Sheol from beneath is moved for thee to meet thee at thy coming, stirring up the dead for thee, all the he-goats of the earth; making to rise from their thrones all the kings of the nations. All of them shall answer and say unto thee, Art thou also become powerless as we; art thou become like unto us? Thy pomp is brought down to Sheol, the voice of thy lyres: the maggot is spread under thee, and worms cover thee. How art thou fallen from heaven, Lucifer, son of the morning! Thou art cut down to the ground, that didst prostrate the nations! And thou that didst say in thy heart, I will ascend into the heavens, I will exalt my throne above the stars of God, and I will sit upon the mount of assembly, in the recesses of the north; I will ascend above the heights of the clouds, I will be like the Most High: none the less art thou brought down to Sheol, to the recesses of the pit. They that see shall narrowly look upon thee; they shall consider thee, saying, Is this the man that made the earth to tremble, that shook kingdoms; that made the world as a wilderness, and overthrew the cities thereof; that dismissed not his prisoners homewards? All the kings of the nations, all of them, lie in glory, every one in his own house; but thou art cast out of thy grave like an abominable branch, covered with the slain — those thrust through with the sword, that go down to the stones of the pit; like a carcase trodden under foot. Thou shalt not be joined with them in burial; for thou hast destroyed thy land, hast slain thy people. Of the seed of evildoers no mention shall be made for ever " (Isa. 14: 9-20). From this it is clear that he designed to place his throne above the angelic assemblies which acknowledged the sovereignty of the Eternal. He sought equality with "the Most High" (contrast Phil. 2: 6). The significance of Satan's reference to God as "the Most High" is indicated in Gen. 14: 18, 19, where the Most High is described as the "possessor of heaven and earth". Lucifer's aim was absolute dominion.

The "north" (Isa. 14: 13) is usually regarded as typical of darkness, as the south is of light and warmth; in relation to the Almighty the reference is to the thick darkness in which He dwells (1 Kings 8: 12). The earthly Zion was "on the sides of the north" (Psa. 48: 2). The astronomer sees a further significance in the north, however. Observation has shown that in the brightest part of the Orion nebula (and Orion is the brightest constellation in the northern sky), in the centre of Orion's sword, there is a gigantic cavern, 16,740,000 million miles wide and at least three times as deep. Dr. E. L. Larkin, the director of Mount Lowe Observatory, says that "masses of gaseous matter, adorned with myriads of glittering points — starry suns, no doubt — form the gigantic walls". Philip Knox, another astronomer, says, "Many believe that if we could look with instruments powerful enough, back into the abyss, this cavern in the skies, we would see the gates of gold, the city of the Eternal King." All this is in the north and it was into "the recesses of the north" that Satan sought to penetrate. But, with the dejected hosts of his followers, the proud Lucifer, the bright shining son of the dawn, was expelled from the immediate presence of God and deprived of the major part of his glory and dignity. Isaiah's prophecy, of course, looks forward to a further experience which still lies in the future (possibly that mentioned in Rev. 20: 1-3), and as Jennings says, "pictures his entry into the unseen world of disembodied spirits. As he enters, the whole concourse of those who have preceded him are pictured as thrilled with excitement, the royal shades . . . spring from their thrones with a cry of astonishment — 'What! Is it possible that thou art become as weak and powerless as we?'" The devil was the original sinner and he has already paid a bitter price for his initial act of wrongdoing.

CHAPTER III

THE EFFECTS OF LUCIFER'S FALL

WHEN God created the earth, "the morning stars sang together, and all the sons of God shouted for joy" (Job 38: 7). It was a scene of beauty and perfection, created for the habitation of the creatures of God's hand. Upon it was erected the dazzling palace of gold and precious gems which was the residence of the exalted "prince of this world", set in an Edenic garden as rich in jewels as the later Eden was in fruit. When, "in the beginning God created the heavens and the earth", the latter was indubitably — like all God's works — the acme of perfection. The inhabitants of that scene of loveliness (of whatever character they may have been — and we are given no details in Scripture) must themselves have been creatures of perfection likewise, and perfect accord unquestionably existed between earth and heaven, maintained by the mighty prince who had the right of access into the Divine presence and could thus link the terrestrial with the celestial by reason of his own privileged position. The title bestowed upon him — Lucifer, the bright, shining son of the dawn — is itself an indication of the light and glory, in the reflection of which his satellites basked, whilst the beneficence of his rule may be inferred from the angelic support apparently attracted by his rebellion. The angels of God deputed to the service of the great ruler doubtless exercised a special ministry in relation to the earth and its original inhabitants and were presumably responsible for the latter's welfare. Happiness and bliss were the lot of God's creatures and blessings abounded on every side.

Yet the second verse of Genesis paints a picture of utter ruin and desolation: "And the earth was waste and empty (tohu v'bohu), and darkness was on the face of the deep." That this was not the original condition, as some commentators have suggested, is evident from Isa. 45: 18, "For thus saith Jehovah Who created the heavens, God Himself Who formed the earth and made it, He Who established it, not as waste (tohu) did He create it: He formed it to be inhabited." The particle vau, translated "and" as the initial word in Gen. 1: 2, may be copulative, disjunctive or adversative, and might equally well be translated "then", or "after", whilst the active verb "was" might reasonably be rendered "became". Pusey asserts that the Hebrew form used in verse 2 effectually detaches it from verse 1 and marks a subsequent condition of things from verse 1. At some date after the first creation mentioned in Gen. 1 : 1, some tremendous cataclysm came upon the earth, which left it in the terrible condition described in the next verse — a condition which, as Isaiah makes clear, was not the original purpose of God. Speaking of a future outpouring of Divine judgment upon the earth, the prophet declares that "He shall stretch out upon it the line of waste (*tohu*), and the plummet of emptiness (*bohu*)". In other words, to quote another writer, the "desolation shall be as complete and shall be exactly measured with the line and plummet of the chaos from which the earth was recalled" in that earlier day (Isa. 34 : 11). The deplorable condition described in Gen. 1 : 2 was evidently the result of Divine judgment and this is corroborated by the Scriptures. Isaiah says, "Jehovah maketh the earth empty, and maketh it waste, and turneth it upside down" (Isa. 24 : 1), and Jeremiah says, "I beheld the earth, and lo, it was waste (*tohu*) and empty (*bohu*): and the heavens, and they had no light" (Jer. 4 : 23), at the same time attributing this state to the fierce anger of Jehovah (see also Job 9 : 4-7).

It has been thought probable by some Bible students that the earth was the sphere of probation, not only for its pre-Adamite occupants, but also for angelic beings, and that the rebellion against the rule of heaven had the earth as its base of operations. It seems likely that this was so and that the fall of Satan and his followers consequently reacted with dire consequences upon the primeval creation. Divine judgment apparently resulted in a complete obliteration of life, and the reduction of a scene of beauty to one of utter chaos and devastation.

The oceans had burst their limits and covered the mountains with floods of destruction; every living thing had been swept to death; the atmospheric moisture had sunk to meet the waters of the deep; and the light of the sun had been completely withdrawn. Satan's dominion had come under the wrath of God. In Job 25 : 5, to quote Cooper, "Bildad asserted that the moon and the stars are contaminated for none of them are pure in the eyes of the Almighty. This is not simply poetry, but the statement of a sober fact. The disorder, the dislocation, and the disarrangement of things generally throughout the universe are a silent testimony of this mighty rebellion, which set in motion forces and powers that corrupted or rendered impure the physical universe." It certainly seems possible that this planet was not the only sufferer in that dreadful hour, and the lifeless condition of the moon today supports the theory that it too came under the wrath of the Almighty because of some link with earth in that prehistoric revolt. No indication is given of the precise manner in which vengeance was meted out: there is simply the record of its awful results. Many expositors take the view that the judgment upon the angelic followers of Satan took the form of their imprisonment in eternal chains in the darkness of the deepest abyss (2 Pet. 2 : 4; Jude 6), but it is extremely doubtful whether these Scriptures have any relevance to the punishment of the rebel spirits of that prehistoric day: indeed, the context suggests that the sin for which the enchainment took place occurred in the Noahic period. Moreover, the later references in Scripture to the activities of evil spirits show that some, at any rate, are still at liberty.

Whether or not there was an immediate punishment of the fallen angels, it is fairly clear that other beings were affected. The command given later to Adam and Eve to " be fruitful and multiply, and fill the earth " (Gen. 1 : 28) was precisely identical with that given to Noah and his sons after the Deluge (Gen. 9 : 1) and is capable of the sense of *replenishing* which is given to it by the Authorized Version. The responsibility of Noah's posterity was to replace the antediluvians who had perished in the flood. By implication, a similar responsibility rested upon our first parents to replace others who had perished. Was there then a pre-Adamite race of men or were there other creatures of which today we have no cognisance? No one can say with certainty, and speculation is fruitless.

There are, in any case, evidences that the sin, which met with its judgment during the period which intervened between the first two verses of the Bible, extended over a considerable period and was not confined to one concentrated act of rebellion. Indeed, the revolt against heaven was, in all probability, the culmination of the sin and iniquity which had developed over a long time and which obviously had become extremely widespread. Pember, for example, writes, " The fossil remains clearly show, not only were disease and death — inseparable companions of sin — then prevalent among the living creatures of the earth, but even ferocity and slaughter." Patently sin existed in this earth in those prehistoric days and the rocks show that even the animal kingdom was affected by it. Disease was rife long before man appeared and was not — as is commonly supposed — directly attributable to Adam's sin. Weather-head points out that "bacteria of the micrococcus and diplococcus orders have been found in coal, in the fossilised remains of the carboniferous era", whilst C. G. Dawson, in *Healing, Pagan and Christian*, says that the earliest example of vertebrate disease due to infection known to scientists is a reptile of 8 million years ago, which broke one of its dorsal spines, the consequent infection giving rise to osteomyelitis. Ages before Adam then, sin had appeared in this planet. (This is, in no way, in conflict with the apostle Paul's statement in Rom. 5 : 12, since that refers to the specific introduction of sin into the human race). The sin of that earlier period was not some mild epidemic, but a disease which had attacked the whole of the inhabitants of the earth. " Since then," continues Pember, " the fossil remains are those creatures anterior to Adam, and yet show evident tokens of disease, death and mutual destruction, they must have belonged to another world, and have a sin-stained history of their own, a history which ended in the ruin of themselves and their habitation. . . . And since a lord and vice-regent was set over the animal kingdom of our world, through whose fall deterioration, disease and death obtained irresistible power over every living creature, so we should naturally conclude that superior beings inhabited and ruled that former world and, like Adam, transgressed the laws of their Creator." The argument is not unreasonable but, at the very least, it can be said that Satan's fall affected even the animal kingdom of that day.

Satan's original dignities included the titles of " prince of the authority of the air ", and " prince of this world ". That he has an aerial kingdom of spirit beings is an unquestion-able fact, but it is equally evident that he had — and has — an authority over the earth. If his aerial kingdom was (and still is) populated by hosts of angelic beings, it is no less reasonable to deduce that his earthly kingdom also had in the beginning (as now) its own population. Those referred to, for example, in Ezek. 28 : 16 as "they" who "filled the midst of thee with violence", may conceivably have been individuals engaged in literal mercantile operations and it may have been their unrighteous "traffic" which corrupted bright Lucifer's earthly "sanctuaries".

Man as now known (*homo sapiens*) is of comparatively recent origin — a fact which is confirmed not only by history but also by statistics of the growth of the population — but no geologist would be prepared to admit that the physical earth first came into being only 6,000 years ago. The long geological ages — the ezoic, palaeozoic, mezozoic, cainozoic and quaternary — demand a history which may well run into millions of years, but if Biblical history is continuous from Gen. 1 : 1, the world was created 60 centuries ago. No reputable scientist could accept such a thesis. Moreover, as Velikovsky points out, "The submersion and emersion of land, the origin of deserts, of gravel, of coal deposits in Antarctica, and the palm growth in the arctic regions; the building of sedimentary rocks; the intrusion of igneous rock above levels containing bones of marine and land animals and of iron in the superficial layers of the earth's crust, the times of geological epochs and the age of man on the earth — all these ask for treatment in the light of the theory of cosmic catastrophism." Some tremendous cataclysm occurred in the earth's history, and the only satisfactory explanation of Biblical cosmogony is that that catastrophic occurrence was during the interval (which was probably an extremely long one) between verses 1 and 2 of Gen. 1. What happened we do not know, but it is clear that Divine judgment fell without mitigation upon the ancient world and wrought unparalleled disaster and destruction upon it. Even a small alteration in the diurnal rotation of the earth would cause hurricanes and tidal waves to devastate the whole earth and to destroy every living thing. Whether by this or by some other means, the Almighty evidently swept the scene of its then occupants, and revealed His intolerant hatred of sin. Proud Lucifer had brought his empire toppling down around him.

CHAPTER IV

THE TEMPTER IN EDEN

SOME time after the judgment of the world for Lucifer's sin, God turned to the planet in its chaotic emptiness and desolation and, in the wonderful six days of divine labour recorded in Gen. 1 : 3-31, He completely reconstructed it and made it fit for the habitation of a new race of creatures. (Whether the "days" were of 24 hours each or were long periods of time is not discussed here). Light shone out over the darkness of the deep; the waters returned to their appointed bounds; land and sea again became separate; the earth brought forth trees and herbs; the sea abounded with fish and the inhabitants of the deep; the air was filled with bird and fowl; the earth received its animal population; sun, moon and stars were revealed in their places, and last of all, the culminating point was reached in the creation of man from the dust of the earth.

Wonderful was this new creature and marvellous was the position in which he was placed. Made in the image of God, receiving into his nostrils the divinely-given breath of life, he was set in authority over all the terrestrial creation. In recognition of his supreme lordship, every living creature came to his feet to receive its name (Gen. 2 : 19). His dwelling was an earthly paradise — the beautiful garden of Eden, with its tree and herb, flower and fruit in rich abundance, with all that might satisfy the human heart or desire. With the single exception of the tree of the knowledge of good and evil, every tree of the garden (including the tree of life) was available to him for food. Of the one tree alone he was commanded not to eat and it was in such a small question of obedience that God chose to make His first test of man.

The great fallen angel had undoubtedly been a silent observer of the tremendous work of reconstruction and creation, and it was presumably with disturbed feelings that he saw the privileged position bestowed upon man. Here was an inferior creature who had not been placed under his jurisdiction and who seemed destined to exercise authority on earth and possibly even to take possession of Satan's own inheritance; doubtless envy and hatred filled the heart of the unseen watcher. "What is man?" asked the psalmist centuries later. "Thou hast made him a little lower than the angels, and hast crowned him with glory and honour" (Psa. 8: 4, 5), but the creature who had now been brought into being was to be the means whereby God would "still the enemy and the avenger" (v. 2). From the moment of his downfall, Satan set himself in opposition to God, and throughout history he has repeatedly attempted to frustrate God's purposes and to overthrow His plans. Knowing the conditions by which the new race had been limited, he immediately sought to ruin man and to draw down judgment upon him, and thereby to disconcert God's purposes of blessing. Before he was allowed to tempt Job, he was compelled to seek permission in the councils of heaven, and it seems probable that similar permission had to be obtained before the Edenic temptation. As in the case of Job, he may have insinuated Adam's inability to resist evil and his consequent unsuitability to supersede the spiritual hosts who were former rulers of the earth.

Satan's approach to Eve was made in the form of a serpent. Many commentators have suggested that the serpent was probably winged in its original condition and that it was at that time free from venom. It was certainly a beautiful animal and Dr. Tayler Lewis says that the word for serpent (*nachash*) was not necessarily derived from the word "to hiss", as is commonly supposed, but possibly from the secondary meaning of that root, "to shine". "This gives, as the first thought in the word for serpent, 'splendour', 'glistening', 'bright', 'shining', either from its glossy appearance or, more likely, from the bright glistening of its eye." It is not without significance that one of Satan's early names was Lucifer, the "light-bearer", or bright and shining one, and 2 Cor. 11: 14 refers to him as "an angel of light" It is also a popular impression that, prior to the fall of man. the serpent moved in an erect attitude. Milton certainly contributed to this belief by his lines in *Paradise Lost*:

> "Not with indented wave
> Prow on the ground, as since, but on his rear,
> Circular base of rising folds that tower'd
> Fold above fold, a surging maze."

As Smith points out, however, "an erect mode of progression is utterly incompatible with the structure of a serpent, whose motion on the ground is beautifully effected by the mechanism of the vertebral column and the multitudinous ribs, which, forming, as it were, so many pairs of levers, enable the animal to move its body from place to place ". On the other hand, the words of the curse plainly imply a change of habit.

Satan took possession of a serpent and appeared to Eve in that guise. Obviously the serpent was a familiar object and one which provoked no fear or the woman would not have tolerated its presence, but sin, danger and fear were yet unknown in Eden's garden. By the combined use of flattery and the instillation of doubt in her mind regarding the terms of the Divine injunction, then of its justification and its true reason, the devil finally enticed the woman to eat of the forbidden fruit. His appeal, as has often been pointed out, was made through every vulnerable point — the lust of the flesh (she saw that the tree was good for food), the lust of the eyes (it was pleasant to look upon), and the vainglory of life (she saw that it was a tree to be desired to make one wise). Only too easily deceived, she not only partook of it herself, but also seduced her husband to do likewise. " The serpent beguiled Eve by his craft," the apostle Paul reminded the Corinthians (2 Cor. 11: 3). The tempter had succeeded and the new creature had failed. But the arch-enemy had counted on justice alone and had ignored the love and mercy which are equally the qualities of the Divine. He must have anticipated immediate judgment and doubtless exulted in the frustration of the Creator's plans and purposes.

God had laid His plans in the ages before the foundation of the world, and the entrance of sin was foreknown and prepared for. In righteousness, He had to expel man from the garden of Eden and to punish him ultimately with physical death, but in that dark hour of human history was given the Divine promise of a Redeemer, in the light of which men walked in faith for four millenniums. After the reluctant confession of sin by Adam and Eve, Jehovah Elohim turned to the serpent and said, " Because thou hast done this, be thou cursed above all cattle and above every beast of the field. On thy belly shalt thou go, and eat dust all the days of thy life. And I will put enmity between thee and the woman, and between thy seed and her seed; He shall crush thy head, and thou shalt crush His heel " (Gen. 3: 14, 15). The serpent had willingly co-operated with the Evil One, and the sentence pronounced upon the irrational animal was perfectly justified. If the curse laid upon it is to be taken literally, there must have been a radical change in the reptile's structure, and Kalisch remarks: "It is agreed that the organism of the serpent is one of extreme degradation; their bodies are lengthened out by the mere vegetative repetitions of the vertebrae; like the worms, they advance only by the ring-like scutes of the abdomen, without fore or hinder limbs; though they belong to the latest creatures of the animal kingdom, they represent a decided retrogression in the scale of beings." Henceforth, all the serpent's food must be eaten from the ground and dust must inevitably be swallowed with the food. No alleviation will be afforded even in millennial days of blessing: even then it will still be true that " dust shall be the serpent's meat " (Isa. 65: 25). There is, of course, an implication that humiliation and degradation were also the future prospect of the arch-enemy who made use of the animal, and the allusion to him in later Scriptures as " the serpent " affords confirmation of this. The terms of the curse pronounced upon the reptile (" be thou cursed above all cattle ") intimate that man's sin had already reacted upon the rest of creation and that the taint — and consequently the curse — had been transmitted to all.

Perpetual enmity was placed between mankind on the one side and the devil and his emissaries on the other. " Satan had deluded Eve into an alliance with himself against the Creator," writes Pember, " but God would break up the confederation ". There was now an open recognition of the enemy and never would Eve again subserve his purposes. The enmity was not restricted to the principals but was to continue between the seed of the serpent and that of the woman. Although the words were spoken to the serpent, they were obviously directed to the one who had possessed himself of the serpent for his nefarious purpose. The seed of the serpent patently includes the evil spirits who are his willing associates, but it also covers those human beings who surrender themselves to his control. " Offspring of vipers," cried John the Baptist as he viewed the Pharisees and Sadduccees coming to be baptised (Matt. 3: 7). " Offspring of vipers," said our Lord later of those who attributed His healing power to an evil source (Matt. 12: 34). " Serpents, offspring of vipers, how should ye escape the judgment of hell?" He asked the hypocritical scribes and

Pharisees (Matt. 23 : 33), whilst He told them plainly on another occasion, " Ye are of your father, the devil " (John 8 : 44). The apostle John also declared that " Cain was of that wicked one " (1 John 3 : 12). Those, therefore, who manifest the same independent pride as Satan and who are motivated by the same spirit as he, are regarded as his seed. There is no dubiety as to the identity of the woman's seed : it was to be One who should crush the serpent's head, and there can be no question that the promised Seed was the Lord Jesus Christ (see also Gal. 3 : 16, where the quotation, however, is from the later promise to Abraham in Gen. 22 : 18). It was significantly to be the Seed of the *woman* and it is pertinent that Christ was born of a virgin and knew no human father (Isa. 7 : 14; Matt. 1 : 23). It is, of course, true that there is a seed which serves Him, which is reckoned to Him for a generation, or posterity (Psa. 22 : 30), but the reference in Gen. 3 : 15 is specifically to Christ Himself.

In the Divine declaration to the serpent lies the first promise to mankind of a Redeemer, and although Adam and Eve were excluded permanently from the scene of earthly bliss, punished with suffering, sorrow and sadness, and compelled to labour for " the bread which perisheth ", they could yet rest in hope of a future redemption of the ruined creation. The prophecy of the bruising of the Deliverer's heel is an intimation of the ignominy, suffering and agony of the crucifixion, but the predicted bruising of the serpent's head is the symbol of the future defeat of Satan and his degradation and eternal banishment to the lake of fire (Rev. 20: 10).

Adam and Eve evidently expected the immediate fulfilment of the promise for, when their first son was born, Eve exultantly called his name Cain (*i.e.* " acquisition "), exclaiming, " I have acquired a man with Jehovah " (Gen. 4 : 1). Her mistake was soon apparent, but it revealed the extent to which she had been convinced of the reliability of the prophecy. It seems fairly obvious that subsequently the difference in character between Cain and Abel led Satan to assume that the younger brother was the promised Redeemer, and that it was at the devil's instigation that Cain murdered his brother. Indeed, the apostle John's statement seems conclusive on this latter point: " Cain was of the wicked one and slew his brother " (1 John 3 : 12).

Satan is permanently identified with the serpent and even

in the last book of the Bible is termed " the ancient serpent, he who is called Devil and Satan " (Rev. 12: 9). " Almost throughout the East," writes Kalisch, " the serpent was used as an emblem of the evil principle, of the spirit of disobedience and contumacy." Deane maintains that the worship of the serpent may be found in most religions. " The progress of the sacred serpent from paradise to Peru," he writes, " is one of the most remarkable phenomena in mythological history, and to be accounted for only on the supposition that a corrupted tradition of the serpent in paradise had been handed down from generation to generation ". Having shown the universality of this worship, he concludes that the Genesis narrative " is powerfully corroborated by the prevalence of this singular and irrational, but natural superstition. Irrational, for there is nothing in common between deity and a reptile to suggest the notion of serpent worship; and natural, because, allowing the truth of the events in paradise, every probability is in favour of such a superstition springing up; for it is more probable that Satan would erect, as the standard of idolatry, the stumbling-block ascertained to be fatal to man. By so doing, he would not only receive the homage he so ardently desired from the beginning but be also perpetually reminded of his victory over Adam, than which no gratification can be imagined more fascinating to his malignant mind." In sacred buildings in some parts of the world is found the hierogram of a circle with wings and a serpent passing through it.

In *The Gentile Nations*, G. Smith says that the worship of the serpent is universal. " Whence, then, did this universal idolatry originate? That it preceded polytheism, is indicated by the attribution of the title Ops, and the consecration of the symbolical serpent, to so many of the heathen deities. The title Ops was conferred upon Terra, Vesta, Rhea, Cybele, Juno, Diana; and even Vulcan is called by Cicero, *Opas*. In Grecian mythology, the symbolical serpent was sacred to Saturn, Jupiter, Apollo, Bacchus, Mars, Aesculapius, Rhea, Juno, Minerva, Diana, Ceres and Proserpine; that is, the serpent was a sacred emblem of nearly all the gods and goddesses. The same remark may be extended to the theogonies of Egypt, Hindustan, and Mexico, in which we find the serpent emblematic, not of one deity, but of many. What, then, is the inference? That the serpent was the most ancient of the heathen gods. The serpent entered into the mythology of every nation; consecrated almost every temple; symbolised almost every deity; was imagined in the heavens, stamped upon the earth, and ruled in the realms of everlasting sorrow. His subtlety raised him into an emblem of wisdom; he was therefore pictured upon the aegis of Minerva, and crowned her helmet. The knowledge of futurity which he displayed in Paradise exalted him into a symbol of vaticination: he was therefore oracular, and reigned at Delphi. The 'opening of the eyes' of our deluded first parents obtained him an altar in the temple of the god of healing; he is therefore the constant companion of Aesculapius. In the distribution of his qualities the genius of mythology did not even gloss over his malignant attributes. The fascination with which he intoxicated the souls of the first sinners, depriving them at once of purity and immortality, of the image of God and of the life of angels, was symbolically remembered and fatally celebrated in the orgies of Bacchus, where serpents crowned the heads of the Bacchantes, and the *poculum boni daemonis* circulated under auspices of the ophite hierogram, chased upon the rim. But the most remarkable remembrance of the paradisaical serpent is displayed in the position which he retains in Tartarus. A cunodracontic Cerberus guards the gates; serpents are coiled about the chariot wheels of Proserpine; serpents pave the abyss of torment; and even serpents constitute the caduceus of Mercury, the talisman which he holds when he conveys the soul to Tartarus. The image of the serpent is stamped upon every mythological fable connected with the realms of Pluto. To such a fearful extent are the presence and image of Satan the destroyer impressed on the wide range of idolatry." The realm of Osiris positively writhes with snakes!

In the minds of some, the serpent will always be associated with the idea of deceit and antagonism to God; in others, it is regarded as the wisest and most intelligent of the animal kingdom. Support for both views is contained in the Genesis story, but whatever credit or discredit attaches to the reptile is due in large measure to the use made by Satan of the serpent in Eden and the early account of the animal there.

CHAPTER V

THE DAYS OF NOAH

AS the years slipped by, sin and wickedness increased with each generation. From Adam's act of disobedience, sin developed into murder in the case of Cain, and into polygamy and slaughter in the case of Lamech (Gen. 4: 23, 24). Judicial functions were not entrusted to man until after the flood, and the age of freedom consequently became one of licence. Cain suffered no capital punishment for his fratricide, and Lamech was able to boast to his wives that no vengeance had overtaken him for his crimes. In the absence of retribution for wrongdoing, there was no deterrent to crime and the inevitable result was moral degeneracy and unparalleled turpitude. The glimpses of the conditions given by the Scriptures and in the mythological accounts of various races reveal that a state of depravity existed which seems almost incredible today. "Jehovah saw that the wickedness of man was great on the earth, and every imagination of the thoughts of his heart only evil continually . . . and the earth was corrupt before God, and the earth was full of violence. And God looked upon the earth, and behold, it was corrupt; for all flesh had corrupted its way on the earth" (Gen. 6: 5, 11, 12). It was, in fact, a cesspool of iniquity.

The prevalent wickedness was not due solely to a natural human decadence and retrogression, however. Its progress had been accelerated by the interposition of apostate spirits who were numbered among the followers of Satan. "When mankind began to multiply on the earth, the sons of God saw the daughters of men, that they were fair and took them wives of all they chose. . . . In those days were the Nephilim on the earth, and also afterwards, when the sons of God had come in to the daughters of men, and they had borne children to them; these were the heroes, who of old were men of renown" (Gen. 6: 1-4). (J. N. Darby says that the word "renown" is better rendered "the name" i.e., they had a peculiar and well-known name in the earth).

It is sometimes maintained that "the sons of God" were simply descendants of the godly Seth and that "the daughters of men" were women of the line of Cain. The latter could hardly be accurate since the word used for " men " is *baadam*, *i.e.*, the Adam, and the reference is clearly to the race of mankind, the descendants of Adam.

In the Septuagint the phrase used in Gen. 6: 2 is " angels of God ". If the " sons of God " were simply the descendants of Seth, the passage suggests, as Pink remarks, that " God's people were limited to the male sex, for the ' sons of God ' were the ones who ' married ' the ' daughters of men ' Again, if the popular theory were true, if these ' sons of God ' were believers, then they perished at the Flood, but 2 Pet. 2: 5 states otherwise — ' Bringing in the flood upon the world of the *ungodly*.' Once more, there is no hint in the Divine record that God had yet given any specific command forbidding His people to marry unbelievers. In view of this silence, it seems exceedingly strange that this sin should have been visited with such a fearful judgment. In all ages there have been many of God's people who have united with wordlings, and have been ' unequally yoked together ', yet no calamity in any wise comparable with the Deluge has followed. Finally, one wonders why the union of believers with unbelievers should result in ' giants ' (Gen. 6: 4)." There cannot be any reasonable doubt regarding the meaning of the Hebrew term translated " sons of God ": it is used only five times in the Old Testament — twice in Gen. 6 and three times in the book of Job (Job 1: 6; 2: 1; 38: 7) — and where used in Job, it obviously relates to angels. It is also found in the singular number in Dan. 3: 25. where Nebuchadnezzar patently referred to a supernatural being. This view is also confirmed by 2 Pet. 2: 4, 5 and Jude 6. Bullinger points out that the word *oiketerion*, translated " habitation " in Jude 6, occurs again only in 2 Cor. 5: 2, where it is translated " house ", *i.e.*, the spiritual resurrection body of 1 Cor. 15: 44. These angels left their spiritual bodies. The phrase " in like manner " in Jude 7 is an adverbial accusative and grammatically links the sexual perversion of Sodom and Gomorrah with the sin of the angels; there is, therefore, strong presumptive evidence that it is illicit union which is in view. Our Lord explicitly stated that the angels in heaven neither marry nor are given in marriage (Matt. 22: 30): they are normally sexless. It was Satan's purpose, however, to contaminate the whole of Adamic womanhood and thereby to prevent the advent of the promised Seed, and it was doubtless at his instigation that angelic beings voluntarily left their aerial habitation and surrendered their dignities and responsibilities in order to commit the impious outrage of cohabiting wth Adam's descendants. Using their inherent power of materialization, they entered into incongruous union with women on earth, the offspring of these unnatural marriages, being " the heroes who were of old, men of renown ".

Mythology is full of incidents reflecting the Scriptural story. Hercules, the powerful giant of antiquity, for example, was alleged to have been born of the illicit union of Zeus and Alcmena. Aztec traditions tell of a race of wicked antediluvian giants of supernatural origin; the Persian sacred books refer to the corruption of the world by Ahriman and the punishment of the people's iniquity by a rainstorm. The apocryphal book of Enoch says that certain angels, divinely set as guards of the earth, were perverted by the beauty of women, whom they taught sorcery, and being banished from heaven, had sons 3,000 cubits high, thus originating a celestial and terrestrial race of demons. Similar traditions are found in North America, Egypt, India and China. It seems clear then that, at the direction of their leader (but also willingly, since their depraved desires had already been fixed upon the women of the earth), a number of angels descended to earth to enter into union with human beings. It has sometimes been thought that the origin of the demons, whose habitat is the air, but who so earnestly yearn for embodiment, is to be found in these unnatural marriages.

There is a curious statement in Gen. 6: 4 that the *Nephilim* (*i.e.*, either " marvellous " or " fallen ones ") were on earth when the irruption of angels took place. It is clear from the construction of the sentence that the Nephilim were not the progeny of the apostate angels, but were quite distinct from these " heroes " or giants (*Gibborim*). A subsequent reference is made to these mysterious beings in Num. 13: 33, "There have we seen the Nephilim — the sons of Anak are of the Nephilim." Quite apart from the angels who entered into union with earthly women, therefore, there were other beings on earth who had fallen from their own estate, and of whom there was a further influx at a later date. These evil beings were doubtless also emissaries of Satan. Judgment presumably fell upon the first group at the flood, and the presence in Canaan of a similar group may well have been one of the reasons for the Divine command that the Canaanites should be extirpated.

The theory has been propounded that the angelic sin began when Adam's daughters reached maturity and continued right up to the deluge and that, after the deluge, there was a further irruption. "We gather from various passages in the Old Testament, particularly from Num. 13 and Deut. 2 and 3," writes Ben Adam, "that when the children of Israel entered Canaan they found the land, in addition to its human population — a population that would have been located there by the scattering of humanity after the flood — contained a super-human population also. These were the Nephilim (fallen angels), and there were various peoples of such gigantic structure that the Israelites were in their own sight as grasshoppers These peoples were variously named, but it is definitely stated that they were originally known collectively as *Rephaim*. . . . The result of the unions between the ' sons of God ' and the ' daughters of men ' was a race of superhuman beings (giants) known collectively as *Rephaim*, and whose existence dates back to long before Abraham, because when he entered Canaan they were already established there as part of the local population." Adam also suggests that special judgment fell upon these unnatural beings and he renders Isa. 26: 14-19 as, "They (*i.e.* the "other lords" of verse 13) are dead, they shall not live; Rephaim do not rise. . . . Thy dead ones shall live; my dead bodies shall arise . . . but the earth shall cast out the Rephaim," and Psa. 88: 10 as, " Shall the Rephaim arise and praise Thee?" His opinion that there is no resurrection for the Rephaim, although logically consistent with his other comments regarding them, will probably seem somewhat far-fetched to some readers, but there is a great deal to be said for his explanation of the origin of the Rephaim.

The condition of the world at this time must have been truly appalling. Profligacy, immorality, infidelity and perversity led to a general demoralisation; bloodshed, violence and hatred destroyed the foundations of established order; angelic iniquity and the intolerable tyranny of the montrous brood sired by the angels completely corrupted the race. Mankind was utterly estranged from God and the supernatural knowledge imparted to him by the angels served only to increase his distance from God. Only one man retained his integrity and loyalty to his Maker in the presence of such gross evil, and for 120 years Noah was a preacher of righteousness. The conditions were graphically described by our Lord, when He said, "they ate, they drank, they married, they were given in marriage, until the day that Noah entered into the ark, and the flood came and destroyed all of them" (Luke 17: 27). So awful was the state of humanity that God removed His guilty creatures by the judgment of the flood. Yet, despite all warnings, their revelry, merriment and licentiousness continued without thought or anxiety right up to the fatal day. Greek mythology states that, in the Iron Age, virtue was entirely displaced by crime, dishonour, violence and hatred, and that, in consequence, Jupiter destroyed mankind with a flood — a statement remarkably similar to that of Genesis. Lenormant says that "the account of the deluge is a universal tradition in all the branches of the human family, with the sole exception of the black race. And a tradition everywhere so exact and so concordant cannot possibly be referred to as an imaginary myth. No religious or cosmogonic myth possessed this character of universality. It must necessarily be the reminiscence of an actual and terrible event, which made so powerful an impression upon the imaginations of the first parents of our species, that their descendants could never forget it."

No retribution fell upon the great arch-enemy who was the author of the angelic irruption and the plan to debauch the human race. On the other hand, men paid for their crimes by physical death, whilst the apostate spirits still face a dreadful future punishment. Even the liberty which these angels possessed after their first expulsion from the celestial heights with their leader was now taken from them and they were imprisoned in darkness to await a coming judgment. "God spared not the angels who had sinned, but having cast them down to the deepest pit of gloom, has delivered them to chains of darkness to be kept for judgment" (2 Pet. 2: 4). Their confinement is stated literally to be in Tartarus. In Greek mythology. Tartarus was the prison of Cronos and the rebel Titans and was a terrible abyss of darkness.

B. B. Wale writes, "Where and what is Tartarus? This is the only place where the word occurs in the Scriptures. What is its meaning? How did the ancient Greeks of the apostle's day use it? What did they understand by it?

Lucian says, 'The *atmosphere* is called Tartarus.' Suidas says, 'It signifies the place in the clouds or in the air.' Parkhurst says, 'It appears . . . that by Tartarus was meant in a physical sense the bounds of this material creation.' Dr. Whateley says, 'The word is to be understood by our dark gloomy earth with its dull clouds, foul vapours and misty atmosphere.' Plutarch says, 'Our air is called Tartarus.' Hesiod and Homer call it the aerial Tartarus. Grotius says, 'That is called Tartarus which is lowest in anything; whether in the earth or in the water or, as here, in the air.' We gather from these testimonies that the word Tartarus signifies the deepest parts of the atmosphere which surround our globe; and likewise the lower parts of the earth. Into this atmosphere the angels (now the demons) were cast who kept not their dignity; in these atmospheric regions, nearest to the earth, they manifestly were when the Lord Jesus Christ was here, though then they were permitted to display their presence, their malice and power more than ever since. . . . That the presence of the devil and his angels in the atmosphere is defiling goes without saying. Job says, 'the heavens are not clean in His sight and He hath charged even his angels with folly'."

Tartarus is obviously only a temporary prison and a more dreadful one lies ahead for these rebellious spirits. "The angels who had not kept their original state, but had abandoned their own dwelling, He keeps in eternal chains under gloomy darkness, to the judgment of the great day" (Jude 6). No indication is given of the number of angels concerned, but it seems evident that it is no small number who are thus confined until the great assize. Others of Satan's hosts may roam at liberty, but the freedom of these has been restricted.

Only Noah and his family were saved from the devastating waters of the flood, and with the subsidence of the waters, it was apparent to the patriarch and his household that they were the sole survivors of the race. "Be fruitful and multiply and fill the earth," came the Divine command (Gen. 9: 1), as previously to Adam and Eve, and the repopulation of the earth has been from Noah's descendants.

In connection with the judgment of the fallen angels and of the corrupt race, some consideration deserves to be given to the difficult question of "the spirits in prison" to whom Peter refers in the following passage, "For Christ indeed has once suffered for sins, the Just for the unjust, that He might bring us to God; being put to death in flesh but made alive in spirit, in which also having gone, He preached to the spirits in prison, heretofore disobedient (or disbelieving), when the long-suffering of God waited in the days of Noah while the ark was preparing" (1 Pet. 3: 18-20). These verses are frequently linked with 1 Pet. 4: 6, "For to this end was the gospel preached to the dead also, that they might be judged, as regards men, after flesh, but live as regards God, after spirit." Those referred to in the latter verse are a larger company than those mentioned in the preceding chapter and patently cover all human beings of any age to whom the Divine message came: they were not merely those who lived in the days of Noah and there is really no connection between the two passages.

The usual interpretation of 1 Pet. 3: 18-20 is that the Spirit of Christ, operating through Noah, preached to men and women in Noah's day who obdurately refused to believe the message and are now dead, but whose spirits are in prison. The Spirit of Christ was in the Old Testament prophets (1 Pet. 1: 11) and it was, of course, by the Holy Spirit that Noah preached (see also 2 Pet. 2: 5 and Gen. 6: 3). This interpretation is based on the assumption that it is the Holy Spirit to whom reference is made in verse 18, and the spirits of dead men in verse 19, but this appears to be fallacious. In the first place, there is no article before "spirit" in the original and it is quite clear that the word stands in direct antithesis to the word "flesh" in the preceding clause. (1 Tim. 3: 16 contains a parallel phrase). Secondly, although the word *pneuma* is used for demons (*e.g.* Matt. 8: 16; Luke 10: 20; 11: 18) and angels (Heb. 1: 7, 14), it is never used of the spirits of men without an express indication that it relates to men: there is no intimation of this in 1 Pet. 3: 19.

Christ came in the flesh, or became incarnate, for the purpose of dying, and He was actually put to death in flesh. He was raised from the dead, however, and the body in which He was raised was a spiritual body and He is now a life-giving spirit (1 Cor. 15: 44, 45). One expositor maintains that His flesh (or body) was in the tomb and that He went in spirit to the prison of the confined spirits. Bengel says, "Christ wrought with the living in His flesh, with the spirits in His spirit."

One fact emerges clearly, *viz.*, that our Lord actually took a journey involving movement from one place to another, for this is what is specifically signified by the word used. C. F. Hogg writes, "This journey was undertaken at a time defined by the context, namely, after His resurrection, and as the word indicates, it had a beginning, a course, and an end. Moreover, it was He, Himself, who undertook the journey. There is no hint that He went by deputy of any kind. The words seem plainly to imply a personal journey here as they certainly do in verse 22, 'having gone into heaven'." In both cases, there was a local motion; as in Eph. 4: 9, 10, the ascent involved a descent.

If the journey was undertaken by our Lord, the preaching was also undertaken by Him and not by Noah acting in His name or by His Spirit. But to whom did He preach? It was clearly to beings who were in existence in antediluvian days and whose disobedience and unbelief were manifested in those days. It is plain that it was their disobedience — and not the preaching — which occurred in the days of Noah. Moreover, the imprisoned spirits, to whom the message came, were evidently spirits at the time of their disobedience and there is, in fact, no evidence in the context that they were at any time anything other than spirits. The verse refers only to "spirits" and not to "spirits of men".

What message could be brought to such? It could not have been the New Testament evangel, since that is solely for mankind (e.g. John 3: 16). But the message preached by Old Testament prophets at times was one of denunciation and judgment and not of mercy and forgiveness. The preaching referred to in Acts 15: 21, for example, was of the law and not of grace. Satanically inspired spirits had committed a crime of such enormity in the eyes of God that they had been plunged down to the depths. To those thus incarcerated, came the Lord Jesus Christ, now risen from the dead, but not to proclaim the possibility of salvation or deliverance from wrath because of His atoning work: there could be no expiation of the guilt of these spirits and no ground of redemption for them. The only message He could bring was of Man's victory and of Satan's condemnation. The Redeemer had come; Satan's plans had been frustrated; the scheming of the centuries had failed; and mankind was now to be reconciled to God. He could proclaim that victory and could declare the inevitability of judgment for the forces of evil, but no other message could He bring for rebels such as these. It was to this limited company in that dread abode that the message came. Whether He, at the same time, liberated the spirits of the believing dead and triumphed over the prisoners in this very act, we do not know. One there was who must have realized the full implications and the great adversary must have been more than ever conscious of the failure of his age-long machinations.

The anonymous authors of *The Computation of 666* contend that Christ descended not merely into Hades or Sheol, but into the pit of the great watery abyss of Abaddon (Rom. 10: 7) and quote Psalms 69, 88 and 130 in confirmation. It is maintained that our Lord's prayer to be saved from the deep mire goes to prove that the waters of the chaos, out of which the cosmos was formed and which overwhelmed it at the flood, are still in existence (see also Luke 8: 31). The suggestion is interesting and ingenious, but it does not seem acceptable.

CHAPTER VI

BABEL

THE judgment of the Flood temporarily removed corruption from the earth, and when the waters had subsided, Noah and his family emerged from the ark to repopulate a cleansed world. " Be fruitful and multiply and fill the earth . . . bring forth abundantly in the earth and multiply therein " (Gen. 9: 1, 7) came the Divine command. There was a tacit implication that the new race should spread to all parts of the world, but a reaction to this soon set in, and a defiant attempt was made to maintain the concentration of mankind in one locality. This counter-action, obviously inspired by the devil in opposition to God's purposes, was led by Nimrod (whose name literally means " rebel "), the son of Cush and grandson of Ham, one of Noah's three sons. Nimrod was also known as Bar-Cush (i.e. son of Cush), or Bacchus. He was " mighty on the earth " and " was a mighty hunter before Jehovah " (Gen. 10: 8, 9). The rapid multiplication of wild beasts provided a constant threat to man's existence in those early days, but the exploits of this mighty hunter and his followers gained him a deserved renown as a deliverer.

Confident of his power and personal strength, Nimrod laid the foundations of the first kingdom of which history knows. His capital was at Bab-el (literally " the gate of God ", although it subsequently acquired the meaning of ' confusion ") in the land of Shinar and there, undoubtedly again at Satanic instigation, he also introduced the beginning of paganism. All pagan mythologies and idolatrous systems show an underlying unity of features, which is strong evidence of their common origin and, in fact, they may all be traced back to the Babylonian mysteries brought into being by this dark king and his beautiful, but infamous, consort Semiramis. This royal pair and their child became the objects of idolatrous worship in very widely separated countries, and they strove to emancipate men from the fear of God and the old patriarchal faith, and to induce them to find their chief enjoyment in sensual pleasures. Their worship in later days was celebrated with Bacchanalian orgies and gross immoralities.

The great rebel was cut off suddenly. Traditions regarding

his death are somewhat confused, but it appears that he was either put to death for apostacy or, more probably, was torn to pieces by a wild boar in the chase. After his death, he was deified under the name of Orion and his widow subsequently claimed that he was the promised seed and that his death was in fufilment of God's prophecy (Gen. 3: 15). The worship of Nimrod was originally practised only in secret, and the Babylonian Mysteries contained many secret rites, which were later transmitted to other countries. The object of this religious system was to bind all mankind in blind submission to the idolatrous priesthood with its royal head. At a later date, Semiramis and her child also found a place among the stars of heaven, and the worship of the queen of heaven and her babe became almost universal — a diabolical imitation, as it was, of what God had revealed. When Babylon was destroyed, Pergamos became the centre of the false religion and, in the apocalytic message to the Church of Pergamos, our Lord referred to the throne of Satan being there and to Satan dwelling there (Rev. 2: 13). Babylon was the fountain-head of idolatry and the scene of one of Satan's greatest victories. A blow was there struck at the patriarchal faith in God, the effects of which are seen in most of the false religions of the present day.

Nimrod was also renowned as the first builder of a city. Instead of encouraging the people to spread over the face of the earth as God had intended, the Babylonian king urged them to settle in a plain in Shinar and to build a city there in which to find shelter from the depredations of the wild beasts. Bricks were made from the argillaceous soil and cemented with bitumen or asphalt. But the building of the city was arrested before it was completed by an amazing occurrence. The people had said, "Come on, let us build ourselves a city and a tower, the top of which is with (or 'has a representation of') the heavens; and let us make ourselves a name, lest we be scattered over the face of the whole earth" (Gen. 11: 4). "Their avowed object was to make themselves a name," says Jacobus. "This was the proud aim of heathenism — to attain to glory without God, by human wisdom and might. The nations henceforth walk in their own ways" (Acts 14: 16). Fuller, with deeper insight, adds that their "object was to found a universal monarchy, by which all the families of the earth, in all future ages, might be held in subjection. . . . Such a scheme must of necessity be founded in ambition; it required union, and, of course, a city, to carry it into execution ". It is probable that this self-willed and disobedient spirit of combination took account also of the necessity for a religious centre in which might be practised the mysteries which had so recently been introduced. Yet this does not fully explain the terms of the Divine assessment of the position. " Jehovah came down to see the city and the tower which the children of men built. And Jehovah said, Behold the people is one, and have all the same language; and this they have begun to do. And now will they be hindered in nothing that they meditate doing " (Gen. 11 : 5, 6). What was the reason for the grave concern indicated by God's words?

The people had commenced to build not only a city, but also a tower, the top of which was to bear a representation of the heavens, and it was evidently this tower which attracted such attention from the Almighty. (The popular impression that the intention was to build a tower to reach to heaven is based upon the unfortunate translation of the A.V. The impossibility of achieving such a feat would have been apparent even at that date.) It is significant that the 153 feet high temple of Birs-Nimrud, which stands near the probable site of the tower of Babel, is built in seven receding stages ornamented with the planetary colours, and is surmounted by a tower, bearing the zodiac and other astronomical figures at its top. The meagre description of the tower of Babel given in Gen. 11 indicates fairly clearly that, upon the summit of the tower, it was intended to inscribe certain astronomical signs and information. Plato says that Adam " was the first to discover the motion of the celestial bodies ", but tradition generally claims that the science of astronomy was invented by Seth; Philo declares that Terah — who was contemporaneous with Noah for over a century and would have had ample opportunity of discussing the subject with him and acquiring the knowledge carried over from antediluvian days — taught astronomy to his son Abraham, who instructed the Egyptians in the science. The knowledge of it possessed by the Greeks and the Romans was almost certainly acquired from the Egyptians. That it was one of the earliest studies of mankind is indisputable and this doubtless partly accounts for the universality of the zodiac signs. Bullinger writes in *The Witness of the Stars*, " If we turn to history and tradition, we are at once met with the fact that the twelve signs are the same, both as to the meaning of their names and as to their order, in all the ancient nations of the world. The Chinese, Chaldean and Egyptian records go back to more than 2,000 years B.C. Indeed, the Zodiacs in the Temples of Dendereh and Esneh in Egypt are doubtless copies of Zodiacs still more ancient, which, from internal evidence, must be placed nearly 4,000 B.C. when the summer solstice was in Leo . . . Cassini commences his *History of Astronomy* by saying, 'It is impossible to doubt that astronomy was invented from the beginning of the world; history, profane as well as sacred, testifies to this truth.' Nouet, a French astronomer, infers that the Egyptian astronomy must have arisen 5,400 B.C. Ancient Persian and Arabian traditions ascribe its invention to Adam, Seth and Enoch. Josephus asserts that it originated in the family of Seth: and he says that the children of Seth, and especially Adam, Seth and Enoch, that their revelation as to the two coming judgments of water and fire might not be lost, made two pillars (one of brick, the other of stone), describing the whole of the predictions of the stars upon them, and in case the brick pillar should be destroyed by the flood, the stone would preserve the revelation ". In other words, from man's earliest days, there was a knowledge, not only of astronomy, but also of the spiritual message of the constellations.

Gen. 1: 14 reveals that the stars were set as signs in the heavens, and Psa. 147: 4 declares that they were named and numbered by God, and Prof. Grimaldi says that " Seth arranged the stars in the sun's apparent course, during the twelve months, into twelve great groups called signs; and Enoch concluded the work by arranging the stars within and without that circle into 36 groups called decans ". The word " zodiac " merely means a path or a way, and refers to the ecliptic circle, or the path of the sun through the stars during the twelve months of the year. The basis of the zodiac is found in the cherubic forms of man, lion, ox and eagle, and these form the four cardinal points, except that the eagle has been made a decan and its place taken by the scorpion. As Bullinger points out, these and all the figures " are perfectly arbitrary. There is nothing in the groups of stars even to suggest the figures. The picture, therefore, is the original and must have been drawn around or connected with certain stars, simply in order that it might thus be remembered and handed down to posterity". The picture itself has its foundation undoubtedly in the promise given to man in Gen. 3: 15, and the signs clearly portray the coming of the Redeemer, His victory and His future glory and triumphant reign. There was no written revelation at that time, but the witness to God and His purposes was to be read in the zodiacal signs. The zodiac is represented as a circle around which are the twelve signs and their 36 decans. The starting-point is indicated by the form of the Sphinx, which has the head of a woman and the body of a lion. The beginning is therefore Virgo, the virgin, and the end is Leo, the lion. The following lines provide a ready way of remembering the signs:

> "First comes the Virgin with the God-given Son,
> Second the Scales declaring man undone,
> Thirdly, we see the hateful Scorpion,
> Mark for the Archer, heaven's victorious One
> The Goat now shows God's resurrection power,
> Aquarius next the stream of life doth pour,
> Then Fishes twain, with band of union,
> Held by the Ram, whose earthly task is done.
> Now note the angry Bull, with blazing eye,
> And next the Twins in heavenly harmony,
> Close followed by the Crab, which tells of rest,
> And last the Lion, the Victor ever blessed."

If the zodiac enshrined a Divine revelation, there could, of course, be no objection to its being preserved. The astronomical information which Nimrod and his rebel followers proposed to inscribe upon their tower must have had some fuller significance that the story of the coming Redeemer. Gen. 1: 14 states that the stars were set in the heavens, *inter alia*, "for signs (*othoth*) and for seasons (*moed*)". The latter term means "appointed time" (see *e.g.*, Gen. 17: 21; 18: 14; 21: 2), and the former "signs" (see Jud. 6: 17). Delitzsch remarks that "an *oth* (from *avah*, to indicate) is a thing, event or act which may serve to guarantee the divine certainty of some other thing, event or act. This happens partly through sensible miracles presently performed (Exod. 4: 8, 9), or through fixed symbols of the future (Isa. 8: 18; 20: 3), and partly through prophesied events, which, whether miraculous or natural in themselves, are not to be humanly foreseen; and therefore if they occur, they authenticate either the divine causality of other events retrospectively (Exod. 3: 12), or their divine certainty prospectively". Among the purposes of the heavenly bodies, therefore, was to indicate events and the relevant cycles or appointed times. In other words, not only was the story of the redemptive work and of future glory written in the pictures of the sky, but other secrets were also enshrined in the pictures. A key was given to the reading of the message God had conveyed, but no key was given to those other secrets and God has forbidden all attempts to pry into them. Astrology was one of man's earliest studies: the Great Pyramid, with its four sides facing the four cardinal points of the compass, for example, was obviously an astrological building. But astrology is a forbidden study, and many are the Scriptural denunciations of it. The prophetic history underlying the zodiacal signs was revealed to Adam by God, but it was never the Divine intention that the knowledge of how to read from the sky the details of the future for the individual or for the company, should come into the possession of unregenrate man. Quite patently, such a knowledge would have rendered man iedependent of God. Such an acquaintance with the occult would have given him absolute power: he would have been able to determine his own future and to decide what action he should take.

From the date and hour of an individual's birth, an astrologer is able to cast a horoscope, but, as another has said, "the difficulty is in its interpretation, i.e. deciding as to the significance of the various planetary combinations which the horoscope reveals." Occasionally an interpretation is remarkably accurate, but our knowledge of the significance of the heavenly bodies nowadays is so resricted that the interpretation of a horoscope is usually little more than sheer guess-work. On the other hand, the amazing correctness in some instances shows quite definitely that astrology is not to be dismissed as completely unreliable or meaningless. It is, however, a science with which man is strictly forbidden to dabble.

The Babel builders had discovered the key to this forbidden occult knowledge. Clearly, it had not been given to them by God. It must have been revealed by Satan — probably through the instrumentality of evil spirits who had descended to earth, or possibly even directly to some individuals who had surrendered themselves completely to the devil's control. The very fact that this knowledge would give man an independence of God would, in itself, be a strong inducement to Satan to convey the information to mankind by some means or other. The followers of the apostate Nimrod, having been "instructed by Satanically-directed evil spirits, had got behind the divine providential plan", writes Adam. "They had torn aside the veil hiding the heavenly administrative method and thus laid bare the whole process. Being able by means of this illicitly acquired knowledge to foresee what the future had in store for them, they could have accommodated their activities thereto — and would have been not only independent of the divine control involved in the administration of the times and seasons, but — the future holding no secrets for them — they would also have constituted themselves individually and collectively the masters of their own fate and the arbiters of their own destiny." It was a most serious position. Moreover, they had foreseen the possibility of some compulsory dispersal of mankind and had, therefore, decided to make some permanent record of the fateful knowledge which had been imparted to them. If they could permanently retain it, they would make themselves a name: they would acquire a renown. They accordingly decided to inscribe the details on the top of the tower they were building, thereby making the information available to future generations as well as to themselves. Well might God say, as He viewed the city and the tower and realized their intentions, "This have they begun to do, and now will they be hindered in nothing that they meditate doing."

Divine intervention was essential and God put an effective stop to man's impudent and impertinent endeavour: any future combined action was rendered absolutely impossible. Up till that time, "the whole earth had the same language, and the same purposes" (Gen. 11 : 1) — the word *d'bharim,* translated "words" in the A.V. is better translated "purposes" (see Neh. 8: 4). "Come, let us go down, and there confound their language, that they may not understand one another's speech," said God (Gen. 11 : 7). In a moment, all their intentions, aspirations and expectations were dispelled and their counsel was brought to nought. The darkness of unintelligibility fell upon them, and their evil machinations were brought to a sudden standstill. The people were scattered and tradition says that the tower was demolished by lightning. One of Satan's most daring schemes had been frustrated, and that in a way which forever prohibited its repetition. Fragmentary knowledge of the occult secrets presumably remained with individuals, but the barrier to discussion and comparison, in addition to the gradual fading from memory, reduced to a minimum the value of such knowledge to the individual.

Up to that time, the land had been in one place (Gen. 1 : 9), but Gen. 10 : 25 reveals that, in the days of Peleg (whose name means " division ") the earth was divided (niphl'gah, i.e. divided by cleavage). Adam writes, " God first separated the people by confounding their language, thus causing them to group themselves according to their respective tongues; He then separated the land — divided it by cleavage. In other words, we get a divinely supervised earthquake. That vast tract of land that formerly had been all in one place was now split up and distributed over the earth's surface in fragmentary fashion. . . . The change in the distribution and configuration of the land was a gradual process. It may have taken a long time. . . . There is nothing necessarily miraculous in either a slow or rapid shifting of land. The miraculous element consisted in the fact of the land being divided according to the dialectic grouping of the people." God's purpose had been that the people should spread over the earth. Satan had sought, not only to corrupt the people, but also to hinder them from populating the whole earth, but the Divine intervention resulted in their scattering, and the Satanic efforts proved completely unsuccessful.

CHAPTER VII

ISRAEL

WITH the rapid increase in the population of the world, there came the inevitable concomitant of an increase in the workings of sin and wickedness. God now began, however, to reveal a little more of His purposes for man, and His dealings commenced — instead of with individuals — with a nation of people, called out by Him to His service and glory (Rom. 9: 4, 5). In accordance with the Divine promises to Abraham, Isaac and Jacob (Gen. 12: 2; 26: 3, 4; 35: 11), the family of Jacob was separated from the nations of the earth. As the purpose of God became apparent, Satanic hostility was demonstrated in attempts to thwart it. Abraham's prevarications regarding his wife (Gen. 12: 11-20; 20: 2-13) and Isaac's regarding his wife (Gen. 26: 7-11), Jacob's deception of his father (Gen. 27: 18-27) and defrauding of his brother (Gen. 27: 36), and other incidents tell of the enemy's endeavours to corrupt the ancestors of the nation and thereby to render it impracticable for a holy God to show His favour to them. Joseph's brethren turned in hatred against him when they conceived that their younger brother might be exalted above them (Gen. 37: 8), and their words possibly led the evil one to conclude that the Divine purposes were centred in Joseph. The devil accordingly instigated the brethren to slay their hated brother (Gen. 37: 20), but this was averted by God's use of Reuben (verse 22). The next attack came upon Joseph's morality (Gen. 39: 7-12), but again his life was preserved. Satan's schemes were brought to naught and the one who entered Egypt as a slave finally sat as supreme ruler, second only to Pharaoh himself (Gen. 41: 43, 44). In due course, Jacob and his sons took up their dwelling in the land of Goshen, basking in the enjoyment of the king's favour and of the privileges of their relationship to Joseph (Gen. 47).

As the descendants of Israel (or Jacob) multiplied very rapidly, they became a source of anxiety to the then reigning Pharaoh and his counsellors. Their prosperity and the success which attended all their undertakings showed that God was with them in blessing and this was sufficient to arouse the devil's suspicion and antagonism. He accordingly stirred up the Egyptians against the elect people. Filled with fear and hatred, the new king placed task-masters over the Israelites, setting the latter specific tasks and duties and reducing them, in effect, to a nation of slaves. Despite hardship and suffering, the affliction of the task-masters, and the rigour of their daily toil, however, Israel still continued to multiply. Their conditions of service were, therefore, worsened and their oppressors became more cruel and embittered, but all to no purpose. Seeing in their preservation and continued survival the evidences of God's protection, and realizing that from this people the promised Seed was to come, Satan redoubled his efforts against them through the instrumentality of the Egyptians. Through his incitation, a decree was issued that all male children born to the Hebrews should be destroyed at birth (Exod. 1: 16). The rigorous and unyielding implementation of this decree would, of course, effectually have brought about the ultimate extermination of the race. Moreover, the Divinely appointed deliverer, Moses, would have lost his life, but through his mother's ingenuity and faith in God, his life was preserved and he was placed in the most favoured position of all.

In each turn of Pharaoh's dealings with Israel is seen the touch of the Satanic hand, but eventually he was forced to release God's people. The deliverance of Israel from the thraldom of Egypt was a display not only of divine grace and mercy, but also of almighty power. The age-long conflict between the forces of good and evil was carried a stage further and Jehovah proved His complete supremacy over Satan and his emissaries.

Every Pharaoh claimed to be an incarnation of the sun-god, Amen-ra, and was popularly known as the son of the sun. He was accorded divine honours and worship in the same manner as the idols which filled the temples of Egypt. Priests, prophets and magicians constantly surrounded him, and the common people bowed low as they paid him homage. Images of the monarch (especially of Rameses 11) occupied temples and became themselves the objects of worship. Not merely to a king, therefore, was Moses commanded to go, but to one who was also a false god, with his false priests and prophets. Very significantly then did Jehovah, the true God, declare to His servant, " I have made thee a god to Pharaoh: and Aaron thy brother shall be thy prophet " (Exod. 7: 1). What the Egyptian falsely claimed to be, God had purposed that Moses should demonstrably be, and He proceeded to prove His power and wisdom through the despised Israelite.

The guardian goddess of Pharaoh was always depicted in the form of a serpent (usually an asp or basilisk), and the king wore a serpent of pure gold on his crown and headdress as a sign that his spirit-protector would destroy anyone who laid sacrilegious hands on the Pharaoh (see *The Encircled Serpent*, by M. O. Howey). Serpents also ornamented his throne and the royal palaces. When the two Israelitish messengers stood before the monarch, the highest significance accordingly attached to Aaron's action as he threw down his rod to the ground and watched its conversion into a writhing serpent (Exod. 7: 10). The Egyptian magicians were by no means nonplussed though. They were experts at the art of snake-charming (which was commonly practised in the East) and at their bidding snakes had frequently become as rigid as a stick and had subsequently reassumed their natural condition. Without difficulty the magicians repeated the miracle (possibly, as on other occasions, it was already a living rod which each had held in his hand) and other serpents crawled before the king. But their triumph was only temporary, since " Aaron's rod swallowed up their rods ". In no unmistakable manner, God had demonstrated the superiority of His power, and had shown clearly that even Pharaoh's guardian goddess was subordinate to Him.

The word *tannin*, translated " serpent ", actually means " dragon " (see Isa. 51: 9 and Ezek. 29: 3) — not without significance when it is recalled that Satan himself is so termed in the Revelation and also that the Egyptian attitude was inspired by him. Trumper suggests that the word should really be translated " crocodile ", in which case, the miracle would be a challenge to the power of the god Sebek and the monster Apep.

Despite the signs and warnings, the king hardened his heart and refused to accede to the request to let the Israelites go. In consequence, the plagues of Jehovah fell upon him one by one, until ultimately, at the loss of his loved son, he bowed to the will of the Eternal and Satan's opposition was thus broken.

The ten plagues, which were inflicted upon Egypt, were not arbitrarily chosen, but were divinely selected with specific purpose, each one being directed against one or more of the false deities in whom the Egyptians trusted. Behind the pagan idols stood evil spirits, subject to the rule of a mighty overlord, and it was against the great adversary himself that Jehovah's hand was ultimately directed. Whilst warning was generally given of the plague which was about to fall, every third plague fell without warning. The first three plagues fell upon the Israelites as well as the Egyptians, and the severity of each was greater than that of its predecessor.

Prof. D. M. Blair has pointed out that "a certain medical sequence runs through a number of the plagues. The first was the turning of the water into blood, an organic fluid which, in that sub-tropical land, quickly became putrescent and stank. Decomposing organic matter is a favourable breeding-ground for many kinds of undesirable life, and there followed the hordes of frogs which developed in the putrid waters. The frogs died and were gathered into decomposing heaps, and the whole land stank. The putrid earth became alive with lice, and these may have been the larval forms of the swarms of flies which followed. Flies are potent carriers of infection and may well have been the vehicles concerned in the spread of septic infections among animals and man in the plagues which next succeeded. To point out this sequence is in no way to belittle the miraculous nature of the plagues. God controlled the time and place in that sequence."

The first two plagues, having been foretold by Moses, were simulated by the magicians. The third plague was not foretold, and the magicians, taken unawares, endeavoured without success to repeat Moses' action.

After the obstinate monarch had been warned of the consequences of his stubborn refusal, the first plague fell upon the country, and the Nile and all the waters of Egypt were turned into blood, and fish died and the water stank. After the summer solstice, the Nile normally becomes red and turbid because of the presence in its waters of minute vegetable growths and animalculae, but this never has the effect of poisoning the fish nor of causing a bad odour. The miracle, however, took place after the winter solstice, the waters were actually turned into blood and not merely reddened, the fish died and a foul smell arose.

The river Nile was the source of Eygpt's prosperity; its fish were the principal food of the poorer people, and upon its inundations depended the harvest. Its streams watered the pleasant gardens of the Egyptians, and nearly every material blessing found its origin in the Nile. The river thus became an object of veneration, its spirit was worshipped as a god, and a maiden was annually sacrificed to it. The river-god Hapi, or Nu, was one of the father-gods of Egypt, and "the judgment upon the river", as one writer remarks, "was no wanton act, but a solemn and striking pronouncement against the folly and blasphemy that ascribed to the river the honour due to God". The plague proved plainly that Jehovah was greater than the river-god and the river. Also associated with the river Nile was the god Osiris, whose deadly enemy was Typhon, a cruel, relentless, evil and vindictive deity, who was always represented as blood-red. Red oxen were sacrificed to him and his symbol of blood defiled those who came near it. The turning of the waters into blood would consequently suggest to the Egyptians the defeat of Osiris by Typhon and the dishonouring of the national religion.

A respite from the plague of blood produced no change of attitude on the part of Pharaoh, and God accordingly struck the land again. "Aaron stretched out his hand over the waters of Egypt; and the frogs came up and covered the land." Frogs are normally harmless and avoid human habitations, but in this instance they swarmed into the houses, beds, ovens, kneading-troughs; in fact, no place was free from them. Eating, cooking, working and sleeping were rendered impossible by these croaking pests. At the height of the Nile's inundation, frogs and toads swarm around the river and the canals, but this was not the period of the inundation.

Again this was no pointless infliction. The frog was a sacred animal and appears on many ancient Egyptian monuments. Small frog images were worn as talismans to protect the individual from evil spirits. It was the symbol of human life in embryo, and Ptah, the creative principle, sometimes took the form of a frog-headed god. Kalisch says that "on very ancient hieroglyphic tablets and on several ancient gems, the frog is represented as sitting on a leaf of the sacred lotus, as a symbol either of the Nile, or of Osiris, the sun. The frogs stood under the authority of the goddess Heki, one of the supreme deities." Heki was the wife of the creator-god; part of her work was to control the frogs and to protect the land from them. The plague revealed clearly that the goddess was powerless against Jehovah. At His word. her alleged restraining influence disappeared and the teeming frogs filled the whole land.

No warning preceded the third plague. Aaron smote the dust with his staff and it at once bred lice throughout all Egypt. The vermin referred to may have been sand-flies, but were more probably the loathsome eastern ticks, which attach themselves to man and beast. The soil of Egypt (the rich alluvial deposit from the annual inundation) was regarded as holy and it was under the protection of another god, Set. But the soil, which the people esteemed as holy, was now breeding these vicious insects. The priests were extremely punctilious in preserving their personal cleanliness: they bathed at least twice a day and shaved their entire body every other day to ensure that no lice or impure thing should defile them and thereby incapacitate them from undertaking their sacerdotal duties. From the sacred dust, however, there now came obnoxious vermin to contaminate them. Set had proved his utter inability to protect either the soil or the priests. Jehovah thus displayed His power over Set and His contempt for the fictitious sanctity of the sacred dust and of the priests of the false gods. Even the magicians were compelled to acknowledge that this was "the finger of God" (Exod. 8 : 19).

For the first time, a distinction was now made in favour of the Hebrews. The houses of the Egyptians were filled with swarms of insects, but Goshen was entirely free. The A.V. states that the swarms were of flies, but there is no confirmation of this: indeed, the terms used suggest rather a mixture of various kinds of insects. Philo indicates that the sand-fly, or gad-fly, was a serious pest in Egypt, but Kalisch considers that the plague was not of flies but of beetles. Swarms of flies would indicate the inability of Beelzebub, the god of flies, to function and control fully, but swarms of beetles would have a still greater significance (quite apart from the destructive power of their serrated mandibles). Amen-ra had a beetle's head, but the beetle was also the emblem of the god Ptah, who was commonly termed "the lord of all the earth". It was also the token of authority : the king and all his important officials wore scarab rings, or rings containing a stone engraved in the form of a beetle. Schwarze suggests that the honour of Aalu, the god of fertile lands and happily occupied dwellings, and Khnemu, the god of buildings, was also affected by this plague. At any rate,

Jehovah showed His superiority over at least Beelzebub, Amen-ra and Ptah.

The fifth plague was a murrain (literally a "pestilence") upon cattle. The ox and the cow were regarded as objects of reverence and as incarnations of the bull-god Apis and the cow-headed goddess Hathor. A live bull was worshipped in several temples as the incarnation of Apis or of Menthu. Now a grievous pestilence — probably a contagious epizootic fever — attacked the sacred cattle and many were slain. In the eyes of large numbers of the people, the implication must have been, not merely that neither Apis nor Hathor were able to defend their own, but that the deities themselves (being incarnate in the animals) had virtually been destroyed. Barnhouse says that "the other domestic animals were sacred also, and the murrain struck the goats and rams, the images of whose heads adorned the bodies of many idols. Even Bubastis, the cat goddess of love, feminine matters and fashion, was scourged with the pestilence." Once again, Jehovah had proved Himself stronger than the pagan deities.

Human beings were burnt alive as sacrifices to the evil deity Typhon or Set and the ashes of the victim thrown into the air with the idea that blessing and prosperity attached to every place where the dust fell. Moses now took ashes and, in the presence of Pharaoh, sprinkled it towards heaven, in mockery of the sacred practice and in defiant challenge of Typhon. Wherever the dust fell, instead of bringing blessing, it produced festering boils and blains. (The word translated "boils" is the "leprosy" of Lev. 13 : 18-20 and "the botch of Egypt" in Deut. 28 : 27, 35.) The priests, stricken with an eruptive disease, were rendered unfit for their functions, and worship of the gods was temporarily brought to a cessation. Moreover, the goddess of the air, Neit, the queen of heaven, became the means of disseminating, not blessing, but disease, and Jehovah again demonstrated the inability of the god and goddess before Him.

Pharaoh being still unbending, God permitted yet a further plague, and in a land which rarely had rain, a terrible hailstorm, accompanied by thunder and lightning, destroyed any unprotected cattle and smote the flax and barley crops. Food, clothing and trade were all affected by this judgment. Shu, the god of the atmosphere, was incapable of controlling the elements. Sekhet, the goddess of fire, instead of preserving from the ill-effects of fire, was found impotent.

Water, fire, earth and air were all objects of worship, but they were all shown now as being subject to Jehovah, whose power was also greater than that of the deities concerned.

The devastations of locusts made them a dreaded pest and, although Egypt seldom suffered from them, devotions were constantly paid to the god Serapis to secure his protection from them. In addition, worship was given to Min, the god of harvests and crops. As a result of the king's obstinacy, however, the land was now covered by millions of locusts and every green thing was destroyed. Supplications to Serapis or Min were completely fruitless; Nepri the grain god and Anubis the guardian of the fields were helpless : Jehovah had proved Himself greater than the gods of Egypt.

The sun-god, Amen-ra, was worshipped by all Egyptians, and Pharaoh was commonly reputed to be an incarnation of the god. In the land of perpetual sunshine, the ninth plague took the form of three days of heavy darkness — a curtain of blackness so thick that it was impenetrable. Amen-ra, the god of the midday sun, was unable to dispel the darkness; Horus, the god of the morning sun, and Tem, the god of the evening sun, were powerless to introduce a gleam of light. Supreme power lay only with Jehovah.

Pharaoh was warned from the beginning of the ultimate consequences of continued refusal to accede to Israel's request (see Exod. 4 : 22, 23). The plagues had been given as additional warnings and also to provide opportunities for repentance and obedience. Since the king remained adamant, God finally inflicted the last of the plagues, and the first-born of men and beasts was slain.

The first-born was sacrificed to the gods and this plague was, therefore, a blow to the prestige of Thoth, the " self-created " god, as well as to Bast, the goddess of life and fruitfulness. The beasts were symbolic of the false deities of Egypt, since almost every god had an animal representation. In the eyes of the people, the son of Pharaoh (who was a god) was also himself a god. None of the gods had been capable of providing protection against the messenger of death, and Jehovah had showed Himself supreme above every false god, and, *ipso facto*, supreme also above the mighty being who inspired and directed the evil spirits behind these pagan deities.

Satan had been defeated in all his manifold manifestations and his subordinate deities had been proved completely

mpotent before God. Pharaoh was forced to release the
people and the devil's plans were thwarted. Even after
their exodus from Egypt, however, the great adversary sought
the destruction of the Hebrews through the agency of the
pursuing hosts of the enemy — only to find himself again
defeated and the armies of Pharaoh overwhelmed by the
waters of the Red Sea (Exod. 14: 27, 28). Following the
redeemed people into the wilderness, the devil succeeded
repeatedly in bringing sin into the camp and his work is
reflected in their murmurings, idolatries and sinfulness. He
may well have anticipated that the idolatrous worship of
the golden calf, for example, would have invoked the Divine
judgment and, but for Moses' intervention, complete
destruction would indeed have come upon them (Exod.
32: 10-14).

Israel's disobedience and rebellion against God, even when
brought into the promised land, reveal Satan's ceaseless and
untiring activity. The history of the Judges and the period
subsequent to Joshua's death is a story of sin, failure and
hoplessness. Seven distinct apostasies are recorded as a
result of Satan's workings.

Again, in the history of the kings, the same story of warfare between the powers of good and evil is found. In the
disobedience and downward path of Saul, in his enmity to
David, in the stains upon David's character, in the rebellion
of Absalom, in the last days of Solomon, in Rehoboam and
Jeroboam and each successive king, there is apparent the
far-reaching power and influence which Satan exerts over
the actions of fallen man. He was early conscious that in
David was the line through which the promised Messiah
must come. Judah had already been marked out (Gen. 49: 10),
and Samuel not only confirmed this but also narrowed the
choice from the tribe to the individual by anointing Jesse's
son as king over Israel (1 Sam. 16: 13). Through Saul, the
devil sought to destroy the man of God's choice, but Jehovah
reserved His chosen through all danger and trial and finally
set him on the throne of Israel, with the promise that his
kingdom should be established for ever, and that Messiah
should proceed out of his loins (2 Sam. 7: 12-16). Even as
king, David knew the attacks of the evil one. On one
occasion, for example, " Satan stood up against Israel, and
moved David to number Israel " (1 Chron. 21: 1), with the

calamitous result that ultimately 70,000 men lost their lives (verse 14).

Throughout the history of the kings, Satan endeavoured to overthrow the descendants of Judah, and in the time of Athaliah, made a determined effort to destroy the whole of the royal house of Judah. Indeed, it was only through the intervention of his aunt, Jehoshabeath, and the fidelity of Jehoiada the priest, that the sole survivor, Joash, was preserved (2 Chron. 22: 10-12). Even earlier, after Jehoram had killed all his brothers, the Arabians killed all his sons except Ahaziah (2 Chron. 21: 4, 17; 22:1). It is impossible not to see the hand of Satan in such happenings. In Esther's day again, he nearly succeeded in wiping out the whole nation (Est. 3: 6, 12, 13; 6: 1).

It was during the life of the Lord Jesus Christ, however, that the devil seems to have exerted the greatest influence upon the people of Israel. It is a sad commentary on the spiritual condition of the nation that he was able to excite their bitterest opposition to their Messiah and ultimately to arouse their passions to such an extent that they could shriek for the blood of God's own Son and choose a murderer in preference to Christ (Matt. 27: 21, 22). Our Lord Himself gave a clue to their condition in words which His hearers never seem to have realized were applicable to the nation, " When the unclean spirit has gone out of a man, he goes through dry places seeking rest; and not finding any he says, I will return to my house whence I came out. And having come, he finds it swept and adorned. Then he goes and takes seven other spirits worse than himself, and entering in, they dwell there; and the last condition of that man becomes worse than the first " (Luke 11: 24-26). Christ was uttering no generalization: He was describing the spiritual condition of the nation of Israel. Farrar writes, " The demon of idolatry had been expelled by the Exile; but had returned in the sevenfold virulence of letter-worship, formalism, exclusiveness, ambition, greed, hypocrisy and hate; and on the testimony of Josephus, the Jews of that age were so bad that their destruction seemed an inevitable retribution." If they had been emancipated from idolatry, they had not turned in repentance and contrition to the true God. They may have ejected a foul intruder, but they had not filled the vacuum thus created; the house was empty and unoccupied (Matt. 12: 44). The inevitable result, as our

Lord pointed out, was that there was a complete inability to resist a further intrusion and the last state was worse than the first. Nor should we decline to take our Lord's words literally. There was unquestionably an unprecedented outbreak of demonic activity during His earthly life and large numbers in the land of Palestine were actually possessed by demons, whilst the subsequent conduct of the nation almost suggests that they were given over nationally to the control of the evil one.

In the early days of the church's history, the Jewish antagonist was regarded by God as devil-inspired and the Lord described the Jewish company which opposed the church of Smyrna as "a synagogue of Satan" (Rev. 2: 9). Their hatred was not merely human passion, but an enmity implanted in them by an invisible power

CHAPTER VIII

THE MESSIAH

WHEN Satan had effected the ruin of the first man, God promised that a Redeemer should come, Who should bruise the serpent's head (Gen. 3: 15). The ensuing centuries tell the story of the devil's determined and unceasing struggle to thwart God's will and to prevent the fulfilment of that promise. When it appeared that Abel was probably the predicted Saviour, Cain was instigated to destroy his brother (Gen. 4: 8). When the race was multiplying rapidly and the difficulty of determining who might be the promised one consequently increased, an attempt was made by the evil one to corrupt the whole race, even to the extent of causing an influx of fallen angels into the world, so that ultimately judgment fell upon a depraved and sinful people (Gen. 6). But God's purpose is never frustrated. When Abel died, another seed was appointed in Seth (Gen. 4: 25). When the Flood wiped out the race, Noah and his family were saved alive.

Abraham's miserable deception (Gen. 12: 11-13; 20: 2), repeated later by his son, Isaac (Gen. 26: 7), the murder of the Hebrew babes (Exod. 1: 16), and many other incidents recorded in the Old Testament are probably all attributable in part to the devil's attempts to nullify the promise of God. As the prophets gradually revealed fuller details of the Coming One — His lineage, birthplace, manner of birth, etc. — the information was doubtless carefully noted by the great enemy of souls and his plans laid accordingly. Repeated endeavours were made to destroy the line through which the Messiah was to come. As already mentioned, on the death of Ahaziah, for example, the whole of the royal house of Judah was exterminated with the exception of a young babe (2 Chron. 22: 10-12), whilst the kingdom eventually ended in the blinding of the captive king and the slaughter of his sons (Jer. 39: 6, 7). On more than one occasion, Satan may well have concluded that the possibility of the royal line producing the Messiah had been reduced to an improbability. But the Almighty is never unprepared and nothing can overthrow His plans.

Prophecy had foretold that a forerunner would precede

the Messiah to prepare His way (Mal. 3 : 1; Isa. 40 : 3). When John the Baptist appeared, it was obvious that he was the one whose coming had been predicted (Matt. 3 : 1-3; Mark 1 : 1-3; Luke 1 : 76-79; 3 : 3, 4; John 1 : 23, *etc.*). It must now have been patent to the adversary that the advent of the Messiah was imminent. Dan. 9 : 25 had indicated the approximate date of His coming; Mic. 5 : 2 had stated His birthplace; and various other prophecies had given additional details.   When the Magi came to Jerusalem, therefore, seeking the new-born King (Matt. 2 : 1, 2), it was not only Herod who marked their mission, and it was doubtless the devil's fear as well as Herod's which led to the massacre of the young children at Bethlehem (Matt. 2 : 16). The assumption that Christ would thus be slain was a misguided one, for the Almighty forestalled Satan, and the Holy Family took refuge in Egypt, thereby fulfilling another prophecy that God's Son should come out of Egypt (Matt. 2 : 15).

As our Lord grew rapidly in favour with God and man, and early demonstrated both His wisdom and His sinlessness, it became very evident to the evil one that the young man who lived in a carpenter's dwelling at Nazareth was none other than the expected Messiah.   All possible doubt was removed by the happenings at Jordan when He was baptised (Mark 1 : 9-11), and the devil immediately set himself to prevent the accomplishment of the work for which Christ had come into the world.   In view of the pre-eminent importance of the matter, he took the step of personally assailing Him and endeavouring, in the greatest and most severe of all temptations, to seduce Him from His loyalty to God and to entice Him to sacrifice the object of His incarnation. Our Lord was led away to the scene of the temptation immediately after His baptism : Matthew says that He " was carried up into the wilderness by the Spirit to be tempted of the devil " (Matt. 4 : 1).   The temptation is commonly thought to have been near Mount Quarantania, on the way to Jericho, a desolate place, inhabited by wild beasts (Mark 1 : 13). The wilderness was said by the Jews to be the abode also of evil spirits and to contain one of the mouths of Gehenna. Christ met the great adversary on his own territory.   The attacks lasted for some 40 days, reaching their climax at the end of this time, and during the whole of that period, our Lord was deprived of food.   " At times of intense spiritual exaltation the ordinary needs of the body are almost suspended," writes Farrar. "But this can only be for a time, and when the reaction has begun, hunger asserts its claims with a force so terrible that such moments are fraught with the extremest peril to the soul. This was the moment which the tempter chose."

At the baptism, the voice of the Eternal declared, "This is My beloved Son" (Luke 3: 22). Satan's first words to our Lord were, "If thou be the Son of God." As in the garden of Eden, he endeavoured — although quite ineffectively in the case of the Second Man — to cast doubt on the reliability of God's statement. Our Lord made no attempt to prove His sonship. He stood there as dependent Man and faced the tempter as Man. The apostle John declares that "all that is in the world, the lust of the flesh, and the lust of the eyes and the pride of life, is not of the Father" (1 John 2: 16), and in these three categories fall all the temptations which can come to mankind. Each of these natural desires was used in the seduction of Eve and each was employed again in the assault upon Christ.

Our Lord was suffering from the pangs of hunger, and the satisfaction of the famished body would have been a perfectly legitimate fulfilment of the "lust of the flesh". Around Him lay stones, which had the appearance of bread (but were in fact only the silicious accretions known as "Elijah's melons"), and which consequently must have served to accentuate the human desire. "If thou be the Son of God, speak that these stones may become loaves of bread," said the tempter (Matt. 4: 3). *Prima facie*, it was entirely reasonable to gratify the natural appetite but, by converting stones into bread, our Lord would have acted independently and insubordinately of His Father God. If it was God's will that He should be temporarily without food and should suffer from the lack, He was content. He declined to consider His own desires or to question His Father's will. He turned upon the tempter with the words, "It is written, Man shall not live by bread alone, but by every word which proceeds from God's mouth" — a quotation from Deut. 8: 3, in which Moses reminded Israel how God had satisfied their hunger with manna, and of their consequent dependence upon Him and of their need for more than physical food. "It is written," as Campbell Morgan says, was "a declaration of the fact that He stood within the circle of the will of God, and what that will permitted, He willed to do; and what that will made no provision for, He willed to do without". He would never exercise the prerogatives of Deity to step outside the circle of the Divine will. No man's life depends upon the bread that perishes: his spiritual life must be nourished by the Word of God. "Man is not merely a fed animal. He is essentially spirit, and spirit depends for its sustenance upon its true correspondence to God." The Master's reply then was not by argument but by the quotation of Scripture, which served as an adequate explication of His position. (The quotation, in each case, coming from the book of Deuteronomy, attested the authenticity and reliability of that book.)

Our Lord's victory in the first temptation demonstrated clearly His absolute confidence in God and it was against this that the next attack was directed. The devil took Him into the holy city (Jerusalem) and set Him upon the pinnacle of the temple — probably on the roof of one of the porches in the southern wing. "If thou be the Son of God," came the subtle voice, "cast Thyself down" — down from the height of the porch-roof to the depths of the dark valley of the Kedron (or possibly of Hinnom) — "for it is written, He shall give charge to His angels concerning Thee, and on their hands shall they bear Thee, lest in any wise Thou dash Thy foot against a stone" (Matt. 4: 5, 6). The words quoted by Satan from Psa. 91 were a temptation to our Lord to demonstrate His confidence in God and in God's commission of Him as Messiah by casting Himself into the abyss. The tacit implication was that His Messiahship would have been convincingly demonstrated and the nation would have accepted Him. But this action would have been to tempt the Almighty, and Christ stripped the suggestion of its speciousness and revealed its true character when He replied, "It is again written, Thou shalt not tempt the Lord thy God" (quoting from Deut. 6: 16). The Divine promise in Psa. 91 was not unconditional, and it would have been impossible to have claimed Divine protection had He deliberately taken Himself out of God's will. Confidence in God is not revealed by bold, adventurous and spectacular actions, but rather by the quiet walk of communion with Him.

Having attacked Christ on the physical and spiritual levels, the evil one made his third assault on a different plane. Taking our Lord up to a high mountain peak, he showed Him all the kingdoms of the world in a moment of time and said, "I will give Thee all this power, and their glory; for it is given up to me, and to whomsoever I will I give it. If, therefore, Thou wilt do homage before me, all of it shall be Thine" (Luke 4: 5-7). It would seem that, in some inexplicable manner, the devil flashed before the Master an amazing vision of the empires of earth, with their splendour and majesty, their peoples and territories, their powers and potentialities, and then offered to bestow them all upon Him in exchange for a simple act of obeisance. There can be no doubt that Satan's claim that they were under his control had some basis in fact: he is the prince of this world and, in a future day, will bestow his earthly authority upon a coming ruler (Rev. 13: 2). On the other hand, God still remains the ultimate and omnipotent suzerain and all power and authority are derived from Him. Again the temptation was not an idle one, for God had promised that the Messiah should receive the nations for His inheritance and the uttermost parts of the earth for His possession (Psa. 2: 8). But the gift was to come from the Divine hand and not from the evil one, and our Lord repulsed him with the words, "It is written, Thou shalt do homage to the Lord thy God, and Him alone shalt thou serve" (see Deut. 6: 13). There was only one supreme Ruler, and Satan's claim to homage was unhesitatingly rejected.

The temptation had failed and the devil was routed. He had tried every possible means of temptation (Luke 4: 13) and had been completely defeated. The Son of Man had withstood all assaults and had used but one weapon — the Word of God. Blandishments and seductions, open assault and subtle attack, had no effect upon One Who was completely dedicated to the service of God, and nothing could cause Him to swerve from the path of allegiance. This severe experience at the commencement of His ministry was not, of course, our Lord's only experience of temptation by Satan: many were the occasions when the devil by various means sought to draw Him aside from the purpose of His life, but every effort was fruitless.

Throughout His earthly life, the Lord Jesus constantly felt the impact of the kingdom of darkness. Surrounding Him were sick and diseased persons, many of them held captive by Satan's subordinates. Demon possession was prevalent throughout Judea, and many of the physical, mental and psychological infirmities, from which He delivered the sufferers, were evidently the result of demonic activity. The Evangelists state plainly that many were possessed with demons (*e.g.*, Matt. 8: 16; Mark 1: 32-34, 39; Luke 4: 41; 7: 21). The madman of Gadara (Matt. 8: 28-33), the dumb man (Matt. 9: 32-34), the blind and dumb (Matt. 12: 22-24), the daughter of the Syrophenician woman (Matt. 15: 22-28), the dumb lunatic boy (Matt. 17: 14-18), the unclean man (Mark 1: 23-27), the woman with spinal curvature (Luke 13: 11), are all examples of cases in which Christ cast out evil spirits. Moreover, our Lord gave His followers power to cast out demons (Matt. 10: 1), and others were also found casting out demons in His name (Mark. 9: 38). Satan's kingdom was threatened by the activities of this Man and His followers. Indeed, when the 70 returned, rejoicing that even the demons were subject to them through their Master's name, the Lord, realising the implication, declared that these were but foreshadowings of Satan's final and conclusive fall from heaven in a future day (Luke 10: 18).

As the wondering crowd saw the Lord expel the demon from the dumb man, some declared that His own power was diabolical — that He cast out demons in collusion with Beelzebub, the prince of demons. The fallacy of the argument was, of course, quite patent. As Willcock pertinently remarks, " Satan would, according to their supposition, have been exerting his power, not only to set this particular person free from his dominion, but to confirm the whole doctrine and precepts of Christ, which were all directly opposed to the kingdom of Satan, and calculated and destined to overthrow it. Such a supposition, therefore, was altogether untenable." A house divided against itself would fall, and if Satan was divided against himself, his kingdom could not subsist. Only one alternative view was possible and the wise Teacher emphasised it, " If by the finger of God I cast out demons, then the kingdom of God is come upon you." Putting the prophecy of Isa. 49: 24, 25 into a different dress, He claimed to be a stronger than the strong man and consequently, to have the power to enter the latter's abode and to spoil him of his possessions and to divide the spoil (Luke 11: 15-22).

Fully cognisant of the danger to his own operations, Satan accordingly asserted himself to the utmost to destroy his great antagonist. He inspired the Pharisees, scribes and priests with anger against Him and on many occasions they would have seized and destroyed Him but for their fear of the populace (see *e.g.* Matt. 21: 45, 46; Luke 6: 11). After His address in the synagogue of Nazareth, they rose up in anger and thrust Him out of the city and, taking Him to the brow of the hill, would have cast Him headlong down the precipice; but the devil's influence was ineffective, for He miraculously passed through the crowd and went His way (Luke 4: 29, 30). Again, as He taught in Solomon's porch, the Jews picked up stones to kill Him, but He escaped out of their hand (Jno. 10: 31-39). All the devil's efforts were unavailing until the Lord's appointed time had come. The evil one even used the Master's own followers in the endeavour to seduce Him from the path which God had set apart for Him. As He spoke of His then future rejection, suffering, and death, Peter said, " Be it far from Thee, Lord : this shall in no wise be unto Thee," but the Lord, recognizing the one who motivated His disciple, at once rebuked Peter, " Get behind Me, Satan : thou art an offence to Me, for thy mind is not on the things that are of God, but on the things that are of man " (Matt. 16: 22, 23). It is sometimes maintained that our Lord merely referred to Peter as an adversary and had no intention of linking him with the powers of darkness, but there is little doubt regarding the meaning of His words. The Saviour had already declared that Satan was at hand when He preached, waiting to snatch away the seed He had sown before it could find root in the heart (Mark 4: 15). One of the most striking examples of the devil's endeavours to destroy Christ was that recorded in Mark 4: 35-41. The Master lay asleep in the stern of His disciples' boat and presently there came a " violent gust of wind, and the waves beat into the ship, so that it was already filled." This was no natural storm, for when He was awakened, He rebuked the wind and said to the sea, " Silence be mute." Unseen inimical powers were at work, which were directing the wind and the sea, and He, who knew the forces of evil, recognised the diabolical attempt.

All efforts to rob Christ of His life were ineffectual until His time came. Then the devil found a willing tool in Judas Iscariot. Judas of Kerioth was an ultra-orthodox Judean whose patriotism yearned for the deliverance of his country from the foreign yoke and for her exaltation above every other race. In Jesus of Nazareth, he thought he recognised the Deliverer of his nation, but the three years of companionship with Him had taught Judas that his Master's ambition was not for an earthly kingdom, and his worldly wisdom foresaw that there could be only one end to the course He pursued. Baffled and bitterly disappointed, Judas turned against his Friend and opened his heart to the foe. Before the Last Supper, the devil had already put it into Judas' heart to betray his Lord (John 13: 2), but the Master gave him the opportunity to repent. As He handed him the morsel from the dish, He revealed to him plainly that He was fully aware of his treacherous intent, but was still waiting to forgive. But then Satan entered into him and recognizing what had happened, Jesus released Judas with the injunction, " What thou doest, do quickly " (John 13: 27). He was " the son of perdition," for whom there was no supplication (John 17: 12). He had opened himself to a supernatural control and Satan's plans were now rapidly coming to fruition. In the garden beyond the river Kedron, the man of Kerioth betrayed his Lord at the dictate of the devil (Matt. 26: 49).

Trial and judgment found no fault in the Perfect Man, but, to satisfy a howling mob and to stave off a Roman official, He was condemned to death. The subsequent crucifixion of the Son of God spelled the apparent triumph of His great adversary; the long-promised Deliverer was expiring in ignominy on a felon's gibbet. The depths of Satanic hatred and malignity were now revealed as never before. In those moments of untold agony for the dying Redeemer, the cross was surrounded not only by visible, but also by invisible foes. Like strong beasts fed upon the rich pastures of Bashan, the Jews gathered round in their brutality and callousness: " great bulls have compassed Me; strong ones of Bashan have beset Me round," their very ferocity revealing their relationship to that other great enemy, for " they opened wide their mouth upon Me, like a lion, tearing and roaring " (Psa. 22: 12, 13). The Gentile dogs, like the unclean, offal-scouring pariahs of the east (1 Kings 14: 11; Psa. 59: 6, 14), heartlessly stood around the cross; " dogs have compassed Me " (Psa. 22: 16). But beyond the visible foes were the deriding and merciless unseen forces of darkness: " an assembly of evildoers have surrounded me " (verse 16) and the great adversary himself, " the lion " (verse 21) was personally present to gloat over his victory. Human comprehension can never grasp the full significance of the sufferings of the darkness. All the hosts of Lucifer gathered around that sacred One, taunting, scorning and insulting the Mighty Maker as His life's blood was poured out for others' sin. The full story of what transpired during those hours will never be known by man on this side of eternity.

It was the hour of Satan's greatest victory. All his plans for the frustration of God's purposes of redemption had apparently been successful and the "Seed of the woman" expired on a Roman cross. But the hour of triumphant victory was converted into the moment of irreparable defeat, and the Conqueror's crown is now justly worn upon the brow of Christ. The serpent may have bruised His heel, but the promise of the Protevangel had been fulfilled — Christ had bruised his head and the final crushing of the evil one was now ensured (Rom. 16: 20). In death, the Saviour faced the one who held the power of death and rendered his power inoperative. He became incarnate, says the writer to the Hebrews, "that through death He might annul him who has the power of death, that is, the devil; and might set free all those who through fear of death through the whole of their life were subject to bondage" (Heb. 2: 14, 15). The devil is here depicted, as Delitzsch remarks, "not as an angel of death appointed as God's messenger in all instances, nor as an arbitrary lord of death, placed in this respect especially over man; but as being one whose dominion is the hidden cause of all dying, not immediately, but mediately, through sin, through which he delivers men over to judicial punishment of death. For death is as much a judicial exercise of God's power as it is a God-hostile exercise of the devil's power by means of sin transmitted from him to men but cherished by them."

Mankind was in the perpetual bondage of fear — the fear of dying — but that fear has now been dispelled and death lies in the power of Christ (1 Cor. 15: 26; Psa. 68: 20). Christ effectively undid the works of the devil (1 John 3: 8). Descending into Hades, He wrested from him the keys of death and Hades and rose triumphantly on the third day, leading with Him a multitude of captives (Eph. 4: 8). There may be an allusion here to the triumphal procession of a conqueror in which the captives take part, and the apostle may have been picturing Satan chained to the chariot wheels of the triumphant Victor. It is certainly true that Christ spoiled the Satanic principalities and powers and made an open show of His triumph over them (Col. 2: 15). It is more probable, however, that the reference is to the release of the souls of the blest from Hades and their carrying into Christ's own presence in heaven. W. E. Vine writes, " The quotation is a forceful expression for Christ's victory, through His death, over the hostile powers of darkness. An alternative suggestion is that, at His ascension, Christ transferred the redeemed Old Testament saints from Sheol to His own presence in glory." Prior to our Lord's death, Hades had evidently been divided into two parts, the abode of the saved (see *e.g.* Luke 16: 22-26). Since the Ascension, paradise is in heaven (2 Cor. 12: 1-4) and believers who die are " with the Lord " (2 Cor. 5: 8) or " with Christ " (Phil. 1: 23). It seems fairly clear that the transference of paradise from Hades to heaven took place at the Ascension and is the event referred to in Eph. 4: 8.

CHAPTER IX

THE CHURCH

THe resurrection and ascension of the Saviour by no means put an end to Satan's activities. A new era commenced in which the eternal purposes of God began to unroll and to reveal hitherto undiscovered plans for mankind. The risen Lord, through the operation of the Holy Spirit, began to call out a people for Himself — a church which was to form a mystical body of which He was the Head, and which was sanctified by the indwelling of the Divine Spirit Himself. National distinctions disappeared and regenerated individuals, whether Jews or Gentiles, were brought into the family of God and made His children. As the new purpose became plainer, Satan must have been filled with jealousy and anger at the privileged position now accorded to creatures of the dust. He had tried by the instrumentality of fear and danger to scatter the disciples after the crucifixion, but the descent of the Holy Spirit at Pentecost and the ushering in of the new era with wonders, miracles and signs, frustrated his endeavours.

The early days of the Church were characterised by constant attacks of the adversary. Through rulers, priests and people, he attempted the destruction of the followers of Christ, but all to no purpose. They were delivered from every assault and the only result was a more rapid spread of the gospel. The very men, who had deserted their Master in His hour of greatest need, now stood intrepidly in the market-place preaching a risen Lord. The devil first sought to remove the leaders of the new movement, and, at his instigation, Peter and John were seized, but only to be released with a warning not to preach (Acts 4: 3, 21). Again the apostles were cast into prison, but an angel opened the doors of the prison for them in the night (Acts 5: 18, 19); Peter was again imprisoned and again miraculously released (Acts 12: 7, 8). The spiritual wisdom and forcefulness of Stephen marked him out as a future leader, and the forces of evil, therefore, temporarily concentrated on him and secured his death (Acts 7: 59). One of the greatest efforts was put forward in the person of Saul of Tarsus, but, at the height of Saul's furious persecution of his people, God intervened and Saul the persecutor was miraculously transformed into Paul the apostle (Acts 9: 1-21). Repeated attempts were made upon the life of this outstanding warrior (Acts 9: 29; 14: 19; 17: 5; 21: 31; 23: 12; 26: 21; 27: 42; 28: 3), but God preserved His servant throughout. Despite all Satan's efforts, the church continued to flourish, and the only result of the persecution seemed to be an increase in the number of converts. During the history of imperial Rome, Satan made a determined effort to wipe out Christianity altogether, but the persecutions of Nero, Domitian, Diocletian and other emperors were without avail. "We sometimes assume," writes Trench, "that Christians were persecuted because the truth for which they bore witness crossed the interests, affronted the pride, would have checked the passions of men, and this is most true; but we have not so reached to the ground of the matter. There is nothing more remarkable in the records which have come down to us of the early persecutions . . . than the sense which the confessors and martyrs, and those who afterwards narrated their triumphs, entertain and utter, that these great fights of affliction through which they were called to pass, were the immediate work of the devil, and no mere result of the offended passions, prejudices or interests of men. The enemies of flesh and blood, as mere tools and instruments, are nearly lost sight of by them in a constant reference to Satan as the invisible, but real author of all." This is particularly exemplified in passages such as Rev. 2: 10.

In the letters to the seven churches in Asia (Rev. 2 and 3), there seems a progressive development in the power of Satan. The church of Smyrna found itself opposed by a "synagogue of Satan" (Rev. 2: 9); the church of Pergamos was reminded that it was located "where the throne of Satan is" and "where Satan dwells" (Rev. 2: 13); but in the church of Thyatira there were apparently some who had known "the depths of Satan" (Rev. 2: 24). The context makes it patent that the reference in the letter to Smyrna was to the Jewish opposition and hatred — undoubtedly inspired by the devil himself — and probably to the Judaising movement which swept so powerfully over the little churches of the east, and which was a deliberate attempt to bring the Gentile convert into bondage to an obsolete Jewish ritual. Pergamos was the centre of the serpent-worship of Aesculapius and was aptly described, therefore, as the place where Satan's throne was and where he dwelt. It was to Pergamos that the high priest and other initiates of the old Chaldean religion fled when Babylon was destroyed, taking with them their sacred vessels and images and the secret teaching regarding the Babylonian mysteries. The serpent was their symbol. Thyatira was suffering from the teaching of gnosticism and, to quote Trench, " in that fearful sophistry wherein they were such adepts, and whereby they sought to make a religion of every courrupt inclination of the natural mind, they talked much of ' depths of Satan ', which it was expedient for them to fathom. They taught that it was a small thing for a man to despise pleasure and to show himself superior to it, while at the same time he fled from it. The true, the glorious victory was to remain superior to it even while tasting it to the full; to give the body all the lusts of the flesh, and yet with all this to main- tain the spirit in a religion of its own, uninjured by them; and thus, as it were, to fight against pleasure with the arms of pleasure itself; to mock and defy Satan even in his own kingdom and domain."

Simultaneously with his endeavours to destroy the church from without, the arch-deceiver attempted its corruption from within. One of the earliest examples was the deceit and prevarication of Ananias and Sapphira. As the former lied to the apostle concerning the proceeds from the sale of his property, Peter discerned the true influence at work. " Why has Satan filled thy heart that thou shouldest lie to the Holy Spirit?" he asked, and the judgment of heaven fell upon the wilful deceiver (Acts 5: 3, 5). Simon the sorcerer would have debased spiritual gifts and brought evil upon the church, but the apostle denounced him for his evil thought (Acts 8: 18-20). Elymas the sorcerer would have turned a seeking soul from the truth, and Peter invoked judgment upon him as a " son of the devil " (Acts 13: 10, 11). Sowing of seeds of discord by the evil one caused division in the Church (see e.g. 1 Cor. 1: 11; 11: 18) and the corruption of individuals brought corruption into the Church (1 Cor. 5: 1; 11: 30).

More subtle and more effective was the introduction — doubtless under Satanic influence — of heretical teachings. Quite early, the churches of the Lycus valley came under the spell of gnosticism and it was not long before these intellec- tual speculations and philosophisings began to permeate other churches. Again, wherever the apostle Paul preached.

Jewish teachers followed him, seeking to fetter the new Gentile converts with the shackles of legalism and Judaism. At the same time, the evil influence affected the Jewish convert and led to widespread apostacy from Christianity. These evidences of Satanic activity were apparent in the first century. The second century saw the publication of the heresy of Montanus, soon followed by Manus, Donatus, Arius and others, the sad story continuing to the present day.

The hand of the evil one was perhaps most clearly seen in the development of gnosticism in the earliest days of ecclesiastical history, since most of the attacks upon the Person of Christ sprang from this teaching. Gnosticism found its origin in dualism — the belief that there were two antagonistic principles, one good and the other evil, "by whose ceaseless action and reaction all visible phenomena are produced." The gnostics believed that the world was framed, not by God, but by a mighty demiurge, who, in the view of some of the gnostic sects, was in opposition to the will of God. These considered that since Adam and Eve were under the dominion of this demiurge, the serpent's incitation to disobedience was a benevolent and not a malevolent act, and was directed to their emancipation. In the view of the Ophites in particular, the Creator was evil and the serpent was the benefactor of the human race. This reversal of the teaching of Scripture — a reversal which must patently have been inspired by the devil — led to the worship of the serpent as divine. One sect, the Cainites, frankly acknowledged Satan as their god and Cain as their first saint. Another, the Euchites, paid divine honours to Satan and propitiated him by doing dishonour to Christ. The Carpocratians of the early part of the second century carried the heretical teaching still farther by maintaining that the Old Testament laws were given by the Evil One and should, therefore, be broken in every detail. The character of these perversions demonstrates what guile and subtlety had been used by the prince of darkness and how effective his machinations proved.

A different mode of seduction made its appearance in the fourth century. In A.D. 324 Constantine the Great declared himself a Christian — to the great rejoicing of God's people — but what seemed to be such a triumph of grace proved subsequently to be a notable and skilfully planned victory for the devil. In the union of Church and State, which resulted from the Emperor's alleged conversion, the Christians found it possible to enjoy both worlds, and Satan began to assume less the character of a "roaring lion" (1 Pet. 5: 8) and more that of an "angel of light" (2 Cor. 11: 14). Today the church is not only divided by sect and schism, but also by unbelief and modernism, while false doctrine continues to spread through the whole body like a noxious plague. At the same time, the evil of the union of secular and spiritual power is still apparent, particularly in countries dominated by the Roman Catholic Church, and to some extent even in the favoured land of Britain. Satan has succeeded only too well. Yet it is still true that it is the presence on earth of the church and of the Holy Spirit who indwells her, which hinders the full manifestation of Satanic power (2 Thess. 2: 6, 7).

The history of the last nineteen centuries reveals his continuing efforts to weaken the Church's testimony to the world and to seduce her from loyalty to Christ. By the introduction of carnality and ambition, discord and strife, heresy and false teaching, clerical and professional distinctions, *etc.*, he has sapped her spiritual strength. When spiritual leaders have arisen, he has inspired opposition against them, and has sought to ensnare and entrap them, and to destroy their influence upon their fellows. It is through the working of the Evil One that ungodly men, who have no personal relationship with the Saviour, have been introduced into pulpit and office, so that the flock is now frequently under the charge of a shepherd who is without spiritual power or knowledge to care for them. The social gospel and philosophical reasonings are — from the devil's point of view — a very satisfactory substitute for the Word of God and deserving of his full encouragement. Yet, in spite of all his apparent successes, and despite the failure, apostasy and weakness of the church, God's plan remains unchanged. In a coming day, He has purposed that there shall be a church in glory without spot, wrinkle, or blemish (Eph. 5: 27). The Christ, who loved the church and gave Himself for her, will yet perfect His work and show the utter failure of the age-long foe. It seems probable that Satan's last assault upon the church, as a collective company, will be at its removal from this scene. His evil cohorts are ranged in their hosts in the air above, and may well threaten the transit of God's people from the earth to heaven, but in order to combat any threatened obstacles, our Lord will personally descend into the air and summon all His redeemed people (1 Thess. 4: 16, 17). No power will be able to stay their progress: the great Head of the Church will personally conduct them home.

Some, like Calvin and De Wette, have seen a reference to the conflict with Satan in our Lord's pledge that the gates of Hades shall not prevail against the church (Matt. 16 :18). Stier, for example, says that "the 'kingdom of death' and the 'kingdom of Satan' are one and the same" and that our Lord's reference was to "His own and the church's certain victory over this strong one ," or Satan. "The gates of death," he maintains, "are not merely entrances but indicate the power of death seizing on his prey and then keeping fast hold of it in his province." It is of course, true, as Schaff remarks, that "the gates of hades, or the realm of death, by virtue of the universal dominion of sin, admit and confine all men and . . . were barred against all return until the Saviour overcame death and 'him that hath the power of death' (Heb. 2: 14) and came forth unharmed and triumphant from the empire of death as conqueror and Prince of life." Lange says, "Throughout the Bible, hades means the kingdom of death; which is indeed connected with the kingdom of Satan, but has a more comprehensive meaning . . . it is figuratively represented as a castle with gates (S. Sol. 8: 6; Job. 38: 17; Isa. 38: 10; Psa. 107: 18). These gates serve a hostile purpose, since they opened, like a yawning abyss of death, to swallow up Christ, and then Peter, or the apostles and the Church, in their martyrdom. For a long time it seemed as if the Church of Christ would become the prey of this destroying Hades. But its gates shall not ultimately prevail — they shall be taken; and Christ will overcome and abolish the kingdom of death in His Church (see Isa. 25: 8; Hos. 13: 14; 1 Cor. 15: 15; Eph. 1: 19, 20). Of course, the passage also implies conflict with the kingdom of evil."

CHAPTER X

TITLES AND POWERS

LUCIFER'S degradation from his lofty position of anointed cherub did not deprive him of all the dignity to which he had been entitled. He still occupies the place of authority to which he was initially appointed and still continues to exercise certain of the prerogatives of power. He is still numbered among " the sons of God " and until the privilege is taken from him in a future day (Rev. 12 : 9) has an access into the presence of God (Job 1 : 6; 2 : 1). So exalted is his position to this day, that even the great archangel, Michael, " did not dare to bring a railing judgment against him " (Jude 9). Jesting and light speaking of spiritual dignities of such eminence, therefore, is not only undesirable and injudicious, but also definitely improper, since all authority is ultimately derived from the Supreme One; and ridicule of authority in the final analysis is ridicule of the Bestower of authority.

In addition to his particular responsibility in relation to the earth, Satan is " the ruler of the authority of the air " (Eph. 2 : 2). Many commentators assume that the apostle's reference to the air was intended to be taken metaphorically and not literally, Beck, for example, says, " The power of the air is a fitting designation for the prevailing spirit of the times, whose influence spreads itself like a miasma through the whole atmosphere of the world. It manifests itself as a contagious nature-power." It is, of course, true that the devil has a very great influence upon the moral and spiritual atmosphere of the world and that mankind generally is affected to a very considerable degree by the " atmosphere " he so subtly creates. He certainly has an authority in that atmosphere, " impregnating it with his own venom, the poisonous vapours of his own dark and godless hell," as Dr. Candlish writes. " The air which the world breathes is under his control; he is the prince of the power of the air; its powerful prince. It is, as it were, compounded, concocted and manufactured by him. Very wisely does he use his power; very cunningly does he compose the air which he would have his victims and subjects breathe. He mingles in it many good ingredients. Even for the worst he does so, making it palpable and seductive. For the lowest company he must needs prepare an atmosphere with something good in it; good fellowship at the least, and a large measure of good humour and good feeling. Then, as a man rises to higher circles, how does he contrive, in the exercise of his princely power, to make the air that is to intoxicate his votaries, or lull them to unsuspecting sleep, all redolent, as it might seem, of good; good sense, good taste, good temper, good breeding and good behaviour, good habits and goodheartedness! Many noisome vapours also that might offend he carefully excludes; so that the inhaling breath perceives nothing but what is pure and simple in what it imbibes and absorbs. But it is the wicked one's air or atmosphere after all. He is the prince of the power of it. He contrives to have it all pervaded with the latent influence of his own ungodliness. His godless spirit is in it all through."

While this is substantially true, it seems fairly evident that Paul's reference was not to the mystical atmosphere from which the sons of disobedience draw their breath, but to the physical atmosphere and to the devil's authority over the spirit realm. The Jewish rabbis taught that the terrestrial atmosphere was Satan's abode and that it was peopled with spirit beings, certain of whom acknowledged his lordship. This is supported by the subsequent statement in the same epistle that "our struggle is not against flesh and blood, but against principalities, against authorities, against the universal lords of this darkness, against spiritual powers of wickedness in the heavenlies" (Eph. 6: 12). Satan does not operate in isolation (Matt. 25: 41): he is the sovereign of hosts of a magnitude which is not normally comprehended (Mark 5: 9) and our Lord Himself referred to him as Beelzebub, the chief of the demons (Luke 11: 18, 19). His very title of "ruler of the authority of the air" implies a well-organized sphere in which subordinates exercise a delegated responsibility under his direction.

The air is the scene of activity of God's invisible ministers, the angels who carry out His commands and serve Him with fear, and whom He uses to protect His own people. In addition, it is populated by apostate angels who are the followers of Satan. Like the elect angels who owe their allegiance to the Almighty, the fallen angels apparently retain their ranks, dignities and titles which were once divinely bestowed upon them — principalities, authorities, lords, *etc.* Those of their number, whose later transgression invoked Divine intervention, are no longer at liberty, but are held in captivity (2 Pet. 2 : 4; Jude 6). There is no hope of redemption for the apostate angels (Heb. 2 : 16), but they will one day be judged by the saints (1 Cor. 6 : 3).

Another class of spirit being also finds a place in the domain of the ruler of the authority of the air, *viz.* the demons. (That there is a difference between angels and demons is indicated in *e.g.* Acts 23 : 8, 9). Of the reality and personality of these subjects of Satan's ethereal hegemony there is adequate testimony in the Scriptures, but no clue is given regarding their origin. The Zend-Avesta declares that they were created by the ruler of the realm of evil (the independent counterpart of the power who presides over the good). It is sometimes suggested that they are the disembodied spirits of pre-Adamite men, or that they are the spiritual progeny (as distinct from the physical) of the unnatural marriages of Gen. 6 : 2, but, in the absence of specific information, this is simply speculation. They are described in various ways in the Bible. In Deut. 32 : 17 and Psa. 106 : 36, 37, for example, there is a reference to the *shedhim* (a term derived from the root *shudh*, to rule or to be lord), who were evidently the spirit-beings behind the idols. (The Assyrian *shedu* denotes tutelary deities). In Lev. 17 : 7; 2 Chron. 11 : 15; Isa. 13 : 21; 34 : 14, *etc.*, the word *seirim* (literally " he-goats ") is used of them. The apostate worship of the *seirim* persisted through the history of Israel until Josiah's reformation (2 Kings 23 : 5-8, where *shearim* should probably read *seirim*), and even in a later day Isaiah depicted them dancing and rejoicing over the ruins of Babylon. In the New Testament, *daimon* and its cognates are the expressions employed. Kurtz and others consider that the term *Azazel* in Lev. 16 : 8-10 can only be the description of an evil demon dwelling in the desert, although Hengstenberg sees no alternative but to regard the term as applying to Satan himself, the sins of the nation being sent back to him. This view, however, is not very logical and we can see no satisfactory explanation of the word.

The personality of demons is clear, as Mrs. Penn-Lewis writes, from " the Lord's direct commands to them (Mk. 1 : 25; 5 : 8; 3 : 11, 12; 9 : 25); their power of speech (Mk. 3 : 11); their replies to Him, couched in intelligent language

(Matt. 8: 29) their sensibilities of fear (Luke 8: 31); their definite expression of desire (Matt. 8: 31); their intelligent power of decision (Matt. 12: 44); their power of agreement with other spirits, and their degrees of wickedness (Matt. 12: 45); their power of rage (Matt. 8: 28); their strength (Mk. 5: 4); their ability to possess a human being either as one (Mk. 1. 26) or as a thousand (Mk. 5: 9); their use of a human being as their medium for 'divining' or foretelling the future (Acts 16: 16); or as a great miracle-worker by their power (Acts 8: 11)." Their depravity and moral turpitude are demonstrated by their actions and by the epithet "unclean" so often applied to them (e.g. Matt. 10: 1; 12: 43; Mk. 1: 23; 5: 2; Luke 6: 18). Frequently they tempt the demonized to unclean thoughts and actions. In some instances, writes Unger, a demon takes possession "for the purpose of sexual gratification and uses every type of uncleanness. This may explain the desire of the possessed to live in a state of nudity, to have licentious thoughts (Luke 8: 27), and to frequent such impure places as tombs. The vile and vicious nature of demons is further demonstrated by . . . their activity in the proclamation of doctrines of free love (1 Tim. 4: 3), with the consequent moral breakdown of an orderly society."

Demons always seek embodiment and are capable of entering the body of man or beast (Matt. 12: 43-45; Mk. 5: 8-13). Seven entered Mary Magdalene (Mk. 16: 9), but a legion (2,000 to 6,000) the Gadarene demoniac (Mk. 5: 9). Apparently they can control both mind and body and are capable of inflicting mental disease as well as physical malady (Matt. 17: 15; Mk. 7: 26; Luke 13: 11), but they seem to possess powers over different parts of the body and are not all possessed of the same powers. The ancient Egyptians believed that a different demon was associated with each of the thirty-six regions into which they divided the human body, but this is an over-simplification. Blindness (Matt. 12: 22), deafness (Mk. 9: 25), dumbness (Matt. 9: 33; 12: 22; Mk. 9: 17), insanity (Luke 8: 26-36), suicidal mania (Mk. 9: 18) and physical deformity (Luke 13: 11-17) are among the ills inflicted by malignant spirits. Their activities differ widely: they may be extremely violent (Matt. 8: 28; Mk. 5: 3-5; Luke 9: 39); they may impart superhuman strength (Luke 8: 29); or they may be subtly seductive (1 Tim. 4: 1). Those cast out by our Lord during

His earthly life acknowledged His authority and recognised Him as the Son of God (Matt. 8: 29; Mk. 3: 11; Luke 4: 41), the Holy One of God (Mk. 1: 24) and Jesus (Acts 19: 15), but our Lord refused their testimony (Mk. 1: 34; Luke 4: 41). They are not ignorant of their future doom and begged our Lord not to bring them into torment before their appointed time (Matt. 8: 29) and not to cast them into the bottomless pit (Luke 8: 31). The Lord Jesus cast them out of their victims by His own power, but His followers exorcised them in the name of Jesus Christ (Acts 16: 18), and this is still practised in cases of demon possession in the mission field today.

All unbelievers are liable to demon possession (Eph. 2: 2), but whilst these evil spirits attack believers, they are incapable of controlling the Christian. W. R. Lewis rightly remarks that "no demon can enter the body of a child of God where the Holy Spirit has taken up His abode, and as regards our conflict with the angelic hosts, full provision has been made for heart and will and understanding". There seems to have been a special irruption of demons into Palestine during our Lord's life and there will be a great irruption out of the abyss in a future day (Rev. 9: 1-3). It should be noted that whilst our Lord recognised the presence and power of evil spirits during His earthly life, He made it perfectly clear that He refused to accept the common superstitions of His contemporaries about them. As Alexander writes, "He commanded His disciples to gather up the fragments; thus discouraging the idea that demons lurk in crumbs. He had no faith in the ceremonial washing of hands; so repelling the notion that spirits may rest on unwashed hands. He asked a draught of water from the woman of Samaria and thereafter entered the city; proving that He had no fear of drinking borrowed water and no belief in local *shedim*. He retired repeatedly to desert places and fasted in the wilderness; therein rejecting the popular conception that the waste is the special haunt of evil spirits."

The "air" in which these spirit beings have their abode is not the entire expanse between earth and heaven, but the atmosphere immediately surrounding the earth. The Greeks distinguished between the lower atmosphere and the more rarefied atmosphere of the mountain-tops, and the word *aer* used in Eph. 2: 2 signifies the lower atmosphere. It is significant that the same word is used in 1 Thess. 4: 17, making it evident that our Lord's descent for His church will be not merely to earth's atmosphere, but to the more immediate vicinity of the earth. He will descend into the hostile territory of the evil spirits and personally remove His church from their presence and power. Satan's hosts are not dispersed through the aerial regions. His original kingdom was on earth and his forces are concentrated around the planet which was once placed in His care.

Three times in the fourth Gospel is Satan described as "the ruler of this world" (John 12: 31; 14: 30; 16: 11). The expression is not used elsewhere, but it was a common designation for Satan in rabbinical writings, save that his rule in this capacity was deemed to be limited to Gentiles and not to extend over Israel. Ignorance of the rabbinical use led to an early suspicion that the use of the title was a tacit support for gnostic theories, and that the person referred to was not Satan but the *demiurgus* by whom allegedly the world was created. The context in each instance, however, makes it clear that it is Satan who was intended. It is sometimes suggested that Satan is a usurper and has no right to the title of "ruler of this world", but the way in which our Lord used the term is a confirmation of the validity of Satan's entitlement.

"Was this world a department assigned to him of God as separate kingdoms have been assigned to different celestial potentates?" asks Torrey. "Did he drag down his dominion with him in his fall?" There is little doubt that this earth was the scene of proud Lucifer's former glory and untimely rebellion, and that it suffered a pre-Adamite judgment as a result of his fall. But it still remains the domain of the great enemy. From his conversation with the Almighty, recorded in Job 1, it is clear that, even yet, he still exercises some sort of supervision over the world. As Pember remarks, the dignity of the ruler of this world, "together with the royal prerogatives, which of right pertain to it, was conferred upon him by God Himself. For there is no other way of explaining the fact that the Lord Jesus not only spoke of the adversary by this title but plainly recognised his delegated authority in that He did not dispute his claim to the present disposal of the kingdoms of the world and their glory. . . . Although Satan is a rebel, he has not yet been deprived either of his title or his power. He is still the Great High One on high who divides the world into different provinces according to its nationalities, appointing a powerful angel, assisted by countless subordinates, as viceroy over each kingdom, to direct its energies and bend them to his will." But that power is still derived from God. As Otto Weininger remarks, "The devil holds his entire power on loan; he knows it and so recognises God as his capital investor; therefore, he revenges himself on God; every act of evil is aimed to destroy the creditor; the delinquent debtor seeks to kill God."

There is ample evidence that spiritual as well as human powers are concerned in the administration of the earth. The Psalmist describes the Divine investigation into the maladministration of the angelic rulers of the earth and the way in which God will inflict retribution upon them for the violence, oppression and flagrant abuses which they have countenanced in their own sphere (Psa. 82). Isaiah also asserts that, in a coming day, God "will punish the host of the high ones on high, and the kings of the earth upon the earth" (Isa. 24: 21), *i.e.* both the spiritual and the human rulers. Again, when the angel of the Lord came forth to speak to Daniel, he was confronted by the rebel spirit princes, whose titles of "prince of Persia" and "prince of Greece" indicated their terrestrial authority (Dan. 10: 20). Behind the human sovereigns are mighty spirits, appointed by Satan, who inspire the actions and programmes of those who visibly govern. The R.S.V. of Deut. 32: 8 (based on the Septuagint and also found in a Hebrew fragment of the passage among the Dead Sea manuscripts) says, "He fixed the bounds of the people according to the number of the sons of God," and Prof. Bruce suggests that there is a clear indication here that God has appointed various angels to preside over the fortunes of the nations.

"The powers that be" are ordained of God but, within the limits set him by the Almighty, Satan is behind the entire system of world government, and powers are but puppets in his hand. He exercises all the rights of sovereignty in a scene which readily subjects itself to him. The greed and ambition of the nations, the diplomacy and deceit of the political world, the bitter hatred and rivalry in the sphere of commerce, the organization of many forms of government itself, the ideologies of peoples, all proceed from a Satanic source. It was the sovereignty over this kingdom

that he offered to Christ (Luke 4: 6), and it is significant
that his right to offer it was not disputed by our Lord.
"Though under the restraining hand of God," writes Chafer,
"Satan is now in authority over the unregenerate world,
and the unsaved are unconsciously organized and federated
under his leading. This federation includes all of the unsaved and fallen humanity; it has the co-operation of the
fallen spirits, and is but the union of all who are living and
acting in independence of God." The Satanic system is
utterly evil and at enmity with God (Jas. 4: 4). It is corrupt
(2 Pet. 1: 4) and polluted (2 Pet. 2: 20). "The whole world
lies in the wicked one" (1 John 5: 19). With the exception
of those redeemed by the Lord Jesus Christ, the entire mass
of men (Jew and Gentile) rest supinely in Satan's embrace.
As B. A. Warburton points out in *Calvinism*, the word for
"evil" in Luke 11: 13 "is not *kokos* but *poneros* and the
words may be rendered, 'If ye then being of the evil one,'
Christ thus asserting that man's fall had placed him under
the dominion of Satan." The death-knell of that mighty
dominion was sounded, however, at Calvary (John 12: 31).

Yet the ambition of Satan has a far greater goal than the
control and direction of the cosmic system or the rule of
mankind in the mass. He has an insatiable desire for the
place of supremacy in man's inmost consciousness. His
original downfall resulted from a determined and deliberate
attempt to place himself on an equality with God and to
attract to himself the homage due to His Creator. That
object has never been surrendered and throughout the
history of the human race he has been endeavouring to
divert religious worship from the true God to himself. "The
god of this age," wrote the apostle Paul, "has blinded the
thoughts of the unbelieving" (2 Cor. 4: 4). It is important
to note that the sin of unbelief is not attributed to him, but
when the individual has declined to believe, the devil is
enabled to becloud his thoughts. "We need not say," writes
Denney, "that the dominion of evil produces unbelief,
though this is true (John 3: 18, 19): or that unbelief gives
Satan his opportunity: or even that unbelief and the blindness here referred to are reciprocally cause and effect of
each other. The moral interests involved are protected by
the fact that blindness is only predicted in the case in which
the gospel has been rejected by individual unbelief." In
order that the glory of the gospel might not shine into the

hearts of such, the devil confuses their thinking and introduces spiritual blindness.

The devilish activity goes farther, of course, than a blinding of the thoughts and far more is conveyed in the title " the god of this age ". It is a common saying that nature abhors a vacuum, and those who reject God consequently need a substitute for Him. Satan accordingly presents Himself as the appropriate object of their allegiance. Not always does he assume a purely religious character : man's worship is often on a lower plane and the object of life is found in the material rather than the spiritual. To some the great enemy therefore becomes the powerful Mammon, the god of money, claiming the affections, desires and energies of many a votary at that shrine; to others he assumes the guise of the Muses or Arts and deludes the beclouded worshippers at another altar; to others he presents himself as fame or honour and draws them away to the pursuit of empty and transient glory; in varying shapes and different forms he appeals to the desires and instincts of man and attracts the individual to himself. Through every idol he erects, he gains the worship of a section of the inhabitants of the world. Behind every phase and facet of man's objects of worship is the central figure of " the god of this age ".

It was the common belief of early Christians that the deities of the ancient pantheons were not meaningless forms evolving initially from the desires and thoughts of those who worshipped them, but were actually representations of powerful spirits, and that the worship of an idol or a false god was worship of an evil spirit who actually existed. " All the gods of the people are idols " (elilim, nothings, empty things), declared the Psalmist centuries ago (Psa. 96: 5), implying that the idols were not realities, but that the demons behind them were the real beings. Since all these invisible forces of evil were subject to Satan, the early church justifiably took the view that all idolatrous worship was, therefore, ultimately directed to Satan himself. The experiences of many a missionary today support the contention that malignant spirits are behind the pagan gods of darkness, and this belief was explicitly confirmed by the apostle Paul when he wrote, " What the nations sacrifice, they sacrifice to demons and not to God " (1 Cor. 10: 20). Moreover, centuries earlier the Psalmist declared that the Israelites sacrificed their sons and daughters to demons when they sacrificed them to the idols of Canaan (Psa. 106: 36-38). In other words, the religions of paganism are not different routes by which men travel heavenwards: they are devilish, and behind the idols of the heathen are the spiritual forces of Satan.

One of the commonest names by which Satan is known in the Scriptures is that of "the devil" (Matt. 4: 1). It is unfortunate that the Authorised Version translates *daimon* as "devil" instead of "demon". The word *diabolos* (accuser or calumniator), which is more properly translated "devil", is the Greek equivalent of the Hebrew name "Satan", or adversary. As Geldenhuys remarks, the name is a reference "to the fact that Satan tries to calumniate the devout before God (as in Job 1 and 2) and, on the other hand, to calumniate God before man (as in the temptation in Paradise and in the temptations of Jesus, where Satan casts reflections on the faithfulness of God). He is constantly striving to make men accept false representations of God". He is the dark spirit who solicits mankind to evil (1 Thess. 3: 5) and who is constantly striving to trap them in his snares (2 Tim. 2: 26).

Although degraded from his former exalted position, he still has access to the heavenlies and periodically appears before the throne of God like the other "sons of God" who have never fallen. Like every other to whom authority is delegated, he has to account to the Eternal for the responsibility entrusted to him. It is clear from the record in Job 1 and 2 that he also uses the opportunity to level accusations against those who are seeking to live godly lives. His accusations are generally well-founded. His opposition to Joshua the high priest was perfectly justified since Joshua was clad in filthy garments (Zech. 3: 3). There is little doubt that every fault and failing, every peccadillo and shortcoming, is carefully recorded by the untiring adversary and recounted in the presence of God. Conscious of his own frailty, the believer might well be disturbed at the ceaseless maligning of his character and life by his bitter foe, but ever in the presence of the Almighty is an Advocate Whose care it is to protect the interests of His own people. Satan's object is to bring the believer into condemnation, but our blessed Lord presents His own plea and the Christian can sing with perfect freedom:

> *" What though the accuser roar*
> *Of ills that I have done ?*
> *I know them all, and thousands more,*
> *Jehovah findeth none."*

The day is not far distant, however, when the accuser will be ejected from heaven and cast down to earth, never again to stand before the Throne as the accuser of the saints (Rev. 12 : 9, 10). It has been suggested that his last appearance there will be at the *bema*, or judgment seat of Christ, when the lives of God's people are assessed and rewards bestowed. It is *possible* that Satan will be present then to draw attention to the faults and failings of believers, but there is no specific Scriptural evidence in support of this idea. He will be ejected from heaven (Rev. 12 : 9) in the middle of Daniel's seventieth week (Dan. 9 : 27), and if this theory is correct, the examination at the judgment seat would occupy three and a half years. Our Lord referred to that future expulsion from heaven in Luke 10 : 18. The seventy disciples had returned, rejoicing that the demons were subject to them in His name. In the subjection of the evil spirits, Christ foresaw the future control of Satan himself and, regarding it potentially as a *fait accompli* (although still future), He declared, " I beheld Satan as lightning falling out of heaven."

Although used of any opponent, whether human or spiritual (see *e.g.* Psa. 109 : 6), the Hebrew term " Satan " is used very frequently as a title of the devil in both the Old and New Testaments (*e.g.* 1 Chron. 21 : 1; 1 Thess. 2 : 18). He is the great antagonist of God's people and their unwearying adversary in all circumstances, but there is the Scriptural assurance that God will soon bruise Satan under the feet of the believer (Rom. 16 : 20).

The devil's first contact with the human race was in the guise of a serpent (Gen. 3 : 1) and it is interesting to note that he is still named as such in the closing book of the Bible (Rev. 12 : 9). The trail of the serpent is traceable throughout history, but reptilian cunning and subtlety will be inadequate to stave off the serpent's long-predicted and inevitable doom.

Our Lord's miracles, particularly in the deliverance of demon-possessed sufferers, were at times so remarkable that His critics declared on one occasion that there could be only one explanation of His supernatural power. He cast out demons by Beelzebub, the chief of the demons (Luke 11 : 15). The folly of the suggestion was perfectly obvious. As our Lord at once pointed out, others had cast out demons and if His own ejection of evil spirits was by the power of the prince of the evil kingdom, the question arose as to the power employed by other miracle-workers: by whom did they cast out demons? The fallacy of the suggestion was patent also from the standpoint of logic. A house divided against itself would inevitably fall and if He cast out demons by the power of Beelzebub, the latter was working against his own aims and interests, which was not very credible.

It is to be noted that our Lord raised no question regarding Satan's right to the title of Beelzebub, and by His tacit acknowledgment of it, He revealed a little more of the extent of the devil's kingdom. The meaning of Beelzebub is not very definite. The comparable name, Baalzebub, was also held by the god of Ekron (2 Kings 1 : 3) and Farrar says, " The Septuagint and Josephus understood the name to mean 'lord of flies'. He may have been a god worshipped to avert the plague of flies on the low sea-coast like Zeus Apomiuos (Averter of flies) and Apollo Ipuktonos (Slayer of vermin). But others interpret the name to mean 'lord of dung', and regard it as one of the insulting nicknames which the Jews, from a literal rendering of Ex. 23 : 13, felt bound to apply to heathen deities. In this place perhaps Beelzebub is the true reading, and that means 'lord of the (celestial) habitation', i.e. 'prince of the air'." This last seems the most likely explanation.

A curious title is given to the great adversary in Job 40 : 15-24, viz. that of Behemoth. While the description in Job is primarily that of a hippopotamus (although some consider it to be a description of an elephant), it is evident that a superior being is also in view, for verse 19 refers to him as "the chief of the ways of God" and there can, in fact, be little doubt that the reference is really to the prince of darkness. In the following chapter (Job 41) is given a description of another fearsome beast, there called Leviathan (v. 1) and probably referring in the first instance to the crocodile (see also Psa. 74 : 14). In Job 41 : 34, however, words are used which are hardly appropriate to a crocodile, " He beholdeth all high things; he is king over all the children of pride." This is an apt description of Satan and, in Isa. 27 : 1, the prophet, in foretelling the future destruction of

Leviathan, identifies this creature with the serpent and, therefore, tacitly with the devil.

In addition to the titles of *Abaddon* and *Appollyon* (Rev. 9: 11), both of which mean "a destroyer", the Apocalypse refers to Satan as "the *Dragon*" (Rev. 12: 3, *etc.*). The dragon was the symbol of pagan Rome: dragons appeared on banners and in the embroidery of imperial robes. But Constantine regarded the devil as a dragon and had a medal struck of himself with a cross, trampling a dragon underfoot, as an indication of his victory over the impious persecutor of the church. Egypt is referred to as a dragon (Ezek. 29: 3), as is also Babylon (Jer. 51: 37), showing clearly that the instruments of Satanic activity are regarded as possessing the same character as the mighty one who inspires them.

In the Old Testament, the name of *Belial* (worthless or lawless) is frequently applied to the Evil One (*e.g.* Deut. 13: 13) and those who follow his dictates are described as "sons of Belial". John refers to him as the father of the wicked (John 8: 38), a liar and the father of lies (John 8: 44), a murderer (John 8: 44), a thief (John 10: 10), a wolf (John 10: 12), and the wicked one (1 John 2: 13), Paul declares that he sometimes masquerades as an angel of light (2 Cor. 11: 14), but Peter refers to him as a roaring lion, seeking whom he may devour (1 Pet. 5: 8).

CHAPTER XI

THE CHRISTIAN'S FOE

GREAT as is the power of our implacable foe, Satan is not the only antagonist with whom mankind — and particularly the followers of the Lord Jesus Christ — is in constant conflict. The cosmic system, in which we live, is controlled by the evil one and is therefore inimical to spirituality and to the maintenance of communion with God. In addition, the inherently sinful nature with which every descendant of Adam is born is a permanent weight from which there is no complete release. Although independent factors, the world and the flesh are closely allied and both only too often subserve the purposes of the great enemy of the soul.

As the ruler of this world, the devil is concerned with the order and organization of the cosmos in all its phases, and since the world-system is completely under his control, its character is anti-Christian and unspiritual. The unconverted walk "according to the course of this world" (Eph. 2: 2), but the world is alienated from God and, therefore, "a friend of the world is the enemy of God" (Jas. 4: 4). Our Lord stated that the world hated Him (John 7: 7) and that He was not of the world (John 8: 23). Hence the believer is enjoined to keep himself "unspotted from the world" (Jas. 1: 27) and to "love not the world, nor the things in the world" (1 John 2: 15). This is more than an abstention from what Plummer describes as "those elements in the world which are necessarily evil, its lusts and ambitions and jealousies, which stamp it as the kingdom of 'the ruler of this world' and not the kingdom of God". It is the refusal to be brought under the domination of a system which is organized and controlled by the devil. The cosmic system may hold much that is intrinsically noble and beautiful and it may appear at times to be organized on the basis of excellent principles, but it is completely out of harmony with God and the true believer finds no pleasure in it. "If any one love the world, the love of the Father is not in him, because all that is in the world, the lust of the flesh, and the lust of the eyes and the pride of life, is not of the Father, but is of the world. And the world is passing away and its lust " (1 Jn. 2: 16, 17). It is, nevertheless, a foe to be feared. Its attractions and allurements are directed to the seduction of the Christian from the path of loyalty to his Master. Its appeal is presented in ways which appear innocuous and perhaps even expedient, but the world is still the enemy of Christ. Through Calvary the world should be crucified to the Christian and he to the world (Gal. 6: 14). Says Perowne, " The world, with its passing interests, its narrowly limited aims, its sordid gains, its perishable treasure, its hollow show, its mockery of satisfaction, is to me like yon felon slave, nailed to the cross, dying by a certain and shameful, if a lingering death." Yet the world is an enemy which can be defeated. " I have overcome the world," said our Lord (John 16: 33), and John triumphantly declares that " all that is born of God gets the victory over the world " through faith (1 John 5: 4).

More firmly entrenched and in many respects more dangerous is the ever-present enemy of man's original nature. Nothing can either change or eradicate that Adamic nature and even conversion does not sanctify it. " In me, that is, in my flesh, no good dwells," said the apostle Paul (Rom. 7: 18) and the Christian finds himself constantly warring against his old nature. His new nature is opposed to the old one, and the flesh and the spirit lust against each other (Gal. 5: 17); the sinful impulses and tendencies of his unregenerate days are still present in his being. Yet Paul declares that the mind of the flesh is death and is enmity against God and that " they that are in the flesh cannot please God " (Rom. 8: 6-8). The flesh, with its desires and longings, is antagonistic to all that is spiritual, and victory is possible only by the crucifixion of the flesh with its passions and lusts (Gal. 5: 24).

In their onslaught upon mankind, Satan and his emissaries make full use of both the world and the flesh. Indeed, in the case of most individuals, there is little need for any intervention by the spiritual forces of evil, since the world and the flesh suffice to engage their full attention. It is doubtful whether Satan takes any action personally against many individuals: in the limited number of cases in which the cosmic system and the Adamic nature are inadequate to defeat the believer, evil spirits are probably deputed to plan the overthrow of the spiritual man. Apparently it is only in the cases of men and women who are of outstanding power in the service of God and whose testimony is vital and far-reaching that the full weight of the deceiver himself is brought to bear. It is customary to say that one was attacked or tempted by the devil but, in the majority of cases, what was experienced was only the striving of the old Adamic nature. Nevertheless, there are exceptional occasions when the adversary himself enters into the fray and brings into use every subtle weapon from his armoury.

" Simon, Simon, behold Satan has demanded to have you, to sift you as wheat," said our Lord to Peter (Luke 22 : 31, 32). Throughout the present age, with Divine permission, believers are still tested and sifted by the devil to prove their faith and to remove the chaff. In this respect, Satan is but serving the purposes of God, and his winnowing has a totally different effect from that which he intends. As Schilder puts it, " His purpose is not to take the chaff from the wheat, but to get the wheat out of the chaff. He wants to shake the disciples so violently that they will lose their minds in the night of fear and anxiety." But the effect of his sifting is, of course, that the chaff is blown away and the wheat remains. " The text discriminates nicely in pointing out that Satan desires this sifting as his *right*, that he files claim to his property now, demands them of God as though he were their owner already. When grain changed hands in the east, the sifting of it became the duty of the buyer, not the seller. . . . Satan acts upon the assumption that he is . . .the owner. The issue does not concern the right to put to the test, to prove, to try the disciples (a sifting designed to bless), nor the right to tempt them (a sifting designed to curse). The basic contention is this : whose *property* are the disciples?" If testing is allowed for the purpose of proving the believer's faith, a Father God ensures that the devil does not go beyond the bounds permitted him, and our Lord Himself assured Peter that He had prayed for him that his faith should not fail. Christ constantly watches over His people, and is ever at hand to supply the grace for seasonable help (Heb. 4 : 16).

Within limitations and subject to the permissive will of God, Satan and his emissaries are able to inflict physical sufferings and maladies upon the people of God as well as upon the unconverted. Job is, of course, an outstanding example of this : not only was the patriarch denuded of family and property but, through the activity of the evil one, health was also snatched away and he sat in misery, covered with boils (Job 2 : 7). But all this was Divinely permitted for Job's refinement and greater blessing (Job 42 : 5, 6). The apostle Paul suffered the buffeting of the devil — " a thorn for the flesh, a messenger of Satan that he might buffet me " (2 Cor. 12 : 7) — in order to preserve him from pride. The devil and his hosts are also used for the chastisement of God's people. For example, Paul declared that he delivered the incestuous man at Corinth " to Satan for destruction of the flesh " (1 Cor. 5 : 5), and again Hymenaeus and Alexander were delivered unto Satan that they might be taught not to blaspheme (1 Tim. 1 : 20). Delivering to the evil one in this way apparently exposes the individual to the infliction of physical and mental sickness. The devil and his forces are also used for the punishment of the ungodly (Psa. 78 · 49). Retribution fell upon the wicked Ahab in this way, since a lying spirit was employed to lead him to disaster at Ramoth-Gilead (1 Kings 22 : 23).

Storms and lightning were attributed to Satanic malignity in Job 1 and the devil's power over the elements was also illustrated in the incident on the lake, when he raised a storm for the purpose of destroying the Son of God (Luke 8 : 22-25).

He operates in the sons of disobedience (Eph. 2 : 2); they are under his control. Moule says, " For illustration of his ' working ', compare the language used of his power on Judas (Luke 22 : 3; John 13 : 2, 27) and Ananias (Acts 5 : 3) and of his energies (through man) at a time of persecution (Rev. 2 : 10). See also 2 Thess. 2 : 9. The subtlety and reality of human personal influence may well prepare us to believe in the mysterious depth and force of Satanic influence, and in the vast variety of its phases from most impalpable to most outrageous."

Prior to the death of Christ, the might of death was also in Satan's hands (Heb. 2 : 14), *i.e.*, not the power to inflict death, but control of the domain of death, but when our Lord rose again from the dead, He broke the power of the adversary and delivered from Hades the souls of the blest (Eph. 4 : 8, *etc.*). With the final resurrection of the dead, death itself will be cast into the lake of fire (Rev. 20 : 14). There is a curious incident recorded in Jude, where the writer says that " Michael the archangel, when disputing with the devil, he reasoned about the body of Moses, did not dare to bring a railing judgment against him, but said, 'The Lord rebuke thee'" (Jude 9). No other information about the incident is given in Scripture. There is a legend that Satan objected to the burial of Moses on the ground that he had slain an Egyptian, but that is patently absurd. Most commentators consider that Moses was buried secretly by God in order that Satan should not induce the people to recover the body for purposes of worship, but this again is not very convincing. It is significant that Moses appeared on the Mount of Transfiguration with Elijah (Luke 9: 30). If it is true that, prior to Calvary, some sort of lien over dead bodies was held by Satan, the preservation of Moses' body out of his grasp was a necessity in the light of the Divine purpose that he should appear at the Transfiguration long after his death.

Satan's power and its effect should not be under-estimated. When he moved David to number Israel, the ultimate result was the death of 70,000 men (1 Chron. 21: 1, 14). He is sufficiently powerful to have been able to hinder Paul on two occasions from visiting Thessalonica (1 Thess. 2: 18). He lays his snares and takes captive his prey (2 Tim. 2: 26). He is one who might well be feared. "Satan is the consummate form of depraved and untruthful intellect," writes Findlay. "We read of his thoughts, his schemes, his subtlety and deceit and impostures (2 Cor. 2: 11; 11: 3; 2 Thess. 2: 9, 10; 2 Tim. 2: 26); of his slanders against God and man (Rev. 12: 7-10; Gen. 3: 4, 5; Zech. 3: 1), from which, indeed, the name devil (diabolos) is given him. Falsehood and hatred are his chief qualities. Hence Jesus called him 'the man-slayer' and the 'father of falsehood' (John 8: 44). He was the first sinner and the fountain of sin (1 John 3: 8). All who do unrighteousness or hate their brethren are, so far, his offspring (1 John 3: 10)." As Barry points out, he does not "act directly and openly, but needs craft and dissimulation in order to get advantage over man by entangling the will. The wiles, the devices, the snares of the devil are expressions which indicate the indirect and unnatural character of the power of evil (Eph. 6: 11; 2 Cor. 2: 11; 1 Tim. 3: 7; 6: 9; 2 Tim. 2: 26)."

Perhaps the outstanding characteristic of the devil is his hatred of God, a hatred which, as Papini says, "derives not only from his first impulse to be independent of God, His grace and His sovereignty. It has grown, little by little, from the recognition that his dependence on his Creator is, even after the fall, eternal. If the devil is still a prince, if power and a kingdom are still his, he owes it only to the will of God who, for His own inscrutable ends, has not destroyed him but has entrusted a realm and a function to him. His awareness of this dependence exasperates him. He is incapable of gratitude. . . . There is in him the secret, profound hatred of the beneficiary for his benefactor. . . . The devil is the bitter, vengeful debtor who uses men as tools in his efforts to rob and wound Him to Whom, even under sentence, he owes everything." He is not so concerned to ruin mankind as, through man's ruin, to strike a blow at the Creator, and this unyielding hatred is behind every action he takes.

CHAPTER XII

LIMITATIONS

THE devil's power, through the hosts of evil spirits who acknowledge his leadership, is far more extensive than is commonly realised. Since they are so numerous, his myrmidons are able to make his influence felt throughout the world, and the deployment of his forces makes it possible to increase or decrease the pressure at any particular part or upon any particular individual or body of individuals as desired. The power of God, however, is far greater than that of the Evil One and the apostle Paul declares emphatically that not even angels, principalities or powers shall separate the Christian from the love of God (Rom. 8: 38, 39). Moreover, despite the extent of Satan's power, such restrictions have been placed by God upon his activities that he cannot boast of freedom to exercise his power. Indeed, in some respects, his limitations at times convert him virtually into an agent of the Almighty, and God does in fact use him for His own purposes (see *e.g.* 1 Cor. 5: 5; Job. 2: 6, 10).

Satan's limitations are very clearly indicated in Scripture. He can touch the possessions, or affect the physical wellbeing of God's people only by the permissive will of God, and he cannot move against the believer without such permission. For example, not until Jehovah had signified that action might be taken, was Satan able to strip Job of material prosperity (Job 1: 12) and he was unable to inflict physical suffering on the patriarch until allowed to do so (Job 2: 6). Even when liberty to act has been afforded to the devil, strict limits are Divinely placed upon the action which may be taken. Our Lord warned the church of Smyrna that Satan would inflict suffering and tribulation upon them, but reassuringly added that the tribulation would last ten days (Rev. 2: 10). The length of the trial was pre-determined: there was a limit set to the time during which Satan could impose trial and tribulation. The God, Who knows the weight which can be borne by His children, never allows a burden which is too heavy nor a temptation which is too great.

There are three attributes which, *in rerum natura*, belong to God alone, *viz.* omnipotence, omniscience, and omnipresence, and no created being possesses these attributes. Although Satan's wicked emissaries make his power felt throughout the world, the fact that he is subject to the will of God and compelled to seek permission before embarking upon certain courses, makes it abundantly clear that absolute power is not his. His initial failure to establish himself on an equality with God, his expulsion from the dignity of the anointed cherub and his future ejection from heaven, all testify to the fact that he is not omnipotent.

His intelligence is probably greater than that of any other living being, but unlimited knowledge and wisdom are not his possession. His lack of knowledge is evident from the errors of judgment which he has made in the course of history, particularly in his endeavours to blot out the line through which Messiah was to come. Even during the present day it is obvious at times that, by taking certain actions, he has over-reached himself — principally because he is not in possession of all the relevant facts or is incapable of forecasting the future. He is definitely not omniscient.

In the Middle Ages it was commonly believed that he was omnipresent. Carducci, for example, says, " Does the poor little nun long for a stalk of endive? In that stalk dwells Satan. Is the monk beguiled by a little bird that sings in his solitary cell? In that song lurks Satan." The operations of the multitude of his followers make the devil's influence felt simultaneously in widely separated places, but he is not personally ubiquitous. When, in Job's day, Jehovah asked Satan whence he came, his reply was, " From going to and fro in the earth, and from walking up and down in it " (Job 1 : 7; 2 : 2), revealing quite plainly that he was not omnipresent. As a creature, he suffers the normal limitations of a creature and can be located in only one place at any moment. God alone is omnipresent and all-pervading.

It is sometimes suggested that Satan is able to enter the thoughts of men and to cause them to think in the way he desires, but this does not appear to be substantiated in fact. By long experience and careful study of the human race during the centuries, he has accumulated an extensive knowledge of normal reactions and can anticipate fairly accurately what thoughts will arise or actions be produced by certain circumstances and particular occasions. This cannot be absolutely precise since there are psychological differences in individuals and reactions are, therefore, not universally uniform. No created being has the power of entering into the thoughts of or reading the mind of another creature, and Satan is no exception to that general rule. At the same time, it cannot be ignored that evil spirits have the power of entering and controlling the bodies of unbelievers and of directing the physical activities of those thus possessed. Quite obviously a closer acquaintance with the mental volitions of the individual is possible in such cases. There is no evidence that evil spirits have the power of entering the bodies of believers.

The greatest check to the exercise of Satan's power on earth is the presence of the Holy Spirit. The full outburst of evil is held under restraint while the Holy Spirit is actually resident on earth, and the devil is unable to implement his plans and programmes unhinderedly. In addition to the restraining power of the Holy Spirit, there is a further hindrance in the presence of the Church which He indwells. Our Lord told His disciples that they were "the salt of the earth": the presence of Christians in the world is still a guarantee against wholesale corruption, and until they are removed, Satan's efforts are limited. It is, moreover, the responsibility of the individual believer to instruct others in the way of Christ in order that they may be delivered from the snare of the devil (2 Tim. 2: 26). In this respect also, the presence of the believer is an embarrassment to the devil.

For the Christian there is a constant and incessant conflict with the forces of evil. "Be vigilant, watch," says Peter. "Your adversary the devil as a roaring lion walks about seeking whom he may devour. Whom resist, steadfast in faith" (1 Pet. 5: 8, 9). In dependence upon the Holy Spirit, there is victory for the child of God over all the powers of evil, and James writes, "Resist the devil and he will flee from you" (Jas. 4: 7). But the strength and subtlety of the foe arrayed against us should never be minimised. "Our struggle is not against flesh and blood, but against the principalities, against the authorities, against the universal lords of this darkness, against spiritual hosts of wickedness in the heavenlies," wrote the apostle Paul (Eph. 6: 12; cf. 2 Cor. 10: 3-5). Evil spirits of all ranks and dignity exert every effort to dislodge those who seek to stand for God, and all "the artifices of the devil" (Eph. 6: 11; the only other N.T. use of this word is in Eph. 4: 14) are used to destroy the believer. Comprehensive and guileful schemes and careful plans are prepared by Satan for the attack (see also 2 Cor. 2: 11), but adequate provision has been made for the Christian's help and protection. "Put on the panoply of God" (Eph. 6: 11) — the most effective guard against Satan's assaults.

In the apocryphal book of Wisdom, it is said that the Lord "shall take His zeal as a panoply, and make the creature His weapon for the defeat of His enemies; He shall put on righteousness as a breastplate, and shall make true judgment His helmet; He shall take sanctity as His invincible shield, and shall whet severe wrath as His sword" (Wis. 5: 17). The prophecy of Isaiah contains a similar passage, "His arm brought Him salvation, and His righteousness, it sustained Him. And He put on righteousness as a breast-plate, and a helmet of salvation upon His head; and He put on garments of vengeance, for clothing, and was clad with zeal as a cloak" (Isa. 59: 16, 17). Doubtless with these quotations in mind, the apostle Paul declares that, if the believer is to be able to stand against the enemy, he must be clad in the panoply of God (Eph. 6: 14-17); nothing else will suffice for this fray, but with this accoutrement, victory is assured.

The loins should be girded with truth, declared the apostle. When action was needed, the flowing robe was tucked into the girdle (Ex. 12: 11; Job 38: 3, etc.). The girdle of the Christian is to be sincerity and reality (cf. Isa. 11: 5); his life is to be upright and free from hypocrisy if he is to gain the victory over the Evil One. The breastplate of righteous-ness (i.e. the wearer's personal righteousness, not the right-eousness of Christ by which he was justified) is to protect his heart (1 Thess. 5: 8): he must have "an approving conscience," says Luther, he must "live a blameless life, injure no one, so that no one may accuse him justly." His shoes are to be the equipment of the gospel of peace (Nah. 1: 15; Rom. 10: 15) and over all, he is to take the shield of faith (the large type of shield used by Roman infantry, which covered the whole body), which is easily turned in any direction to quench the fiery darts shot at him by the Wicked One (a reference to the darts which carried burning material and caused painful wounds). "These fiery darts," writes Stoeckhardt, "refer to specific Satanic temptations. . . . Cruel doubts, scruples of conscience, burning self-accusations . . . they are mortal weapons which will drive the Christian to despair and ruin if he does not resist with utmost power." The shield of faith stops and quenches the darts. "By faith we present Christ and His blood, through which our sins are atoned for, against the assaults of the devil." The helmet of salvation is also provided to protect sight and mind (1 Thess. 5: 8). The Christian's salvation is assured, and he is protected from attacks by this very certainty. No armour is provided for the back, since it is never contemplated that the believer will do aught but face the foe. Only one offensive weapon is supplied, "the sword of the Spirit, which is the Word of God". "God's Word originates from the Spirit, the Spirit creates the Word and operates through the Word," writes Stoeckhardt. "It is just because of this that the Word of God is a victorious weapon." It is significant that this was the sole weapon used by our Lord in His temptation. With the equipment provided for his protection, the Christian need never be overcome by the forces of evil.

There is no reason for defeat. At Calvary, the Lord Jesus Christ met the adversary and overthrew him: Satan is a defeated foe, and the victory of Christ nearly two millennia ago is potentially the Christian's victory today. The rejoicing saints of the Apocalypse overcame the accuser by the blood of the Lamb and by the word of their testimony (Rev. 12: 11). The victory of Calvary is the pledge that Satan will ultimately be overthrown, and the blood of Calvary is a check upon his power today.

There is an additional reason for assurance inasmuch as the Lord Jesus Christ stands in heaven as intercessor, adding His own incense to the prayers of the saints, and rendering them efficacious before the throne of God (Rev. 8: 3, 4). However great the power of the devil below, there is One above Whose thoughts are ever upon His people. Failure and sin, temptation and difficulty cannot separate us from Him.

> "When Satan tempts me to despair,
> And tells me of the guilt within,
> Upward I look and see Him there,
> Who made an end of all my sin."

CHAPTER XIII

THE WORSHIP OF SATAN

FROM the earliest days of the human race, it seems to have been generally realised that Satan and his innumerable spirit hosts possess a far-reaching power for evil, and the fear thereby induced in the hearts of men naturally prompted them to seek ways of propitiating the forces of darkness. Instead of relying upon the protection of God and paying their allegiance to Him, therefore, it became much more customary to bring offerings to appease the evil spirits and to gain their friendship instead of their enmity. To this day, Shiva, the destroyer, is worshipped equally with Brahma and Vishnu in India; again, American Indians recognise not only the Great Spirit, who is good, but also inferior evil deities, who must be propitiated to avoid calamity; additionally, in many parts of Africa, sacrifices and ritual tell of the innate dread of the powers of evil.

Quite apart from religious observances and offerings which spring from fear, there has also been through the centuries a ready and voluntary worship of the prince of darkness. The ancient Oriental belief in dualism resulted in worship being paid to the evil power as well as to the good, since both were regarded as possessed of divinity and equal power. In certain gnostic sects of the first century, by a strangely perverse reasoning, Satan was worshipped as God directly by the Cainites and indirectly (in the guise of the serpent) by the Ophites. The teaching which gave rise to this is now reappearing, as the following extract from *The Secret Doctrine* by H.P.B. shows: " So little have the first Christians . . . understood the first four chapters of Genesis in their esoteric meaning, that they never perceived that not only was no sin intended in this disobedience, but that actually the ' Serpent' was the ' Lord God' Himself, who as the Ophis, the Logos, or the bearer of divine creative wisdom, taught mankind to become creators in their turn. They never realised that the Cross was an evolution from the ' tree and the serpent', and thus became the very first fundamental symbol of creative cause." It seems incredible that some should be so deluded as to believe that Satan was the source of good, but such delusion well serves the ends of the evil one. Others, recognising that the devil was evil and antagonistic to the Almighty, have deliberately allied themselves with him and served him with blasphemous rites because they believed that they had been deserted by God. In many parts of the world there are openly avowed devotees of the devil, many of whom adore him in the form of a serpent. The Yezidis of Iraq, for example, believe that Satan (or Shaitan) was expelled from heaven, but given authority over the earth and, therefore, sacrifice to him regularly at the Temple of the Black Serpent at Sheikh Adi.

The worship of Satan has always been accompanied by a calculated parodying of sacred things. In most instances, the cross was singled out for dishonour, being fastened upside down or being used as a doormat to be trampled upon. Black candles took the place of white ones, black hangings surrounded the walls of meeting-places, and images of the evil one were placed above the altar. In some cases the body of a nude woman was used as an altar. Christian worship was mocked in every detail. Blasphemous liturgies were used, and the forces of evil adored in vile and ribald hymns. The Mass was celebrated in reverse as a "Black Mass" and consecrated elements were frequently stolen for the purpose and defiled before use. Many stories are told of children being slain and their flesh used in the celebration, their blood being mingled with the wine of communion. It was the normal practice, after the evil ritual had been carried out, for all lights to be extinguished — with the inevitable result that the scene soon became a saturnalia of promiscuous debauchery. A group discovered at Orleans in 1022 A.D. were sent to the stake because of their blasphemous and obscene practices, but Satanism has never been blotted out; indications of its continued existence have appeared throughout the centuries right up to the present day.

In the 13th century a large tribe of Frisian peasants called the Stedingers gave themselves over completely to the service of the devil and became so utterly corrupt and vicious as to constitute a public menace. Pope Gregory said of them, "The Stedingers, seduced by Satan, have abjured all laws, human and divine; they have derided the church, insulted and horribly profaned the sacraments; consulted with witches to raise evil spirits; shed innocent blood like water; burned and plundered and destroyed; they are in fine enemies to all good, having concocted an infernal scheme to propagate the cult of the Devil, whom they adore at their secret sabbats." Eventually they revolted against the civil authorities and were crushed by the Duke of Brabant in 1234 A.D., 8,000 being killed and the rest scattered. "There was a widespread cult of witchcraft in the sixteenth and seventeenth centuries and a ritualistic ceremony connected with it in which the Devil was worshipped. The initiates were sworn to secrecy, but they doubtless did their best to spread horror and superstition among the simple country people. At the numerous witch trials of the time, the accused seemed proud of their claims to have had dealings with the Devil, who they said, changed them from time to time into a hare, the better to carry out his malicious undertakings. One of the most notorious spots for the holding of the sabbat was the village of Zugarramurdi, in the Basque country. Near it is a great cave in which the orgies took place. They were presided over by the He-Goat and accompanied by the frenzied dancing of the assembled company. In 1610, in the city of Logrono, the suspects of Zugarramurdi were rounded up and tried *en bloc* by the Inquisition."

In *The Sons of the Valley*, the German poet Werner reveals that the Order of the Knights Templar in the following century was rotten with Satanism. Secret gatherings were held, at which a grotesque idol, called the Baphomet, formed the principal object of adoration, whilst the cross was subjected to desecration and the devil was worshipped. In *The Brethren of the Cross*, E. A. M. Lewis says that the noble knights expected the reinstatement of Satan to be effected by the deposition of Christ. The Templars are alleged to have been the real founders of the Society of the Luciferians, which spread through France, Italy and Switzerland, and which early assumed a political, as well as religious (or anti-religious) character. Prof. Robison, Abbé Barnuel and other historians show conclusively that the French Revolution was carefully and methodically engineered by these votaries of Satan, and, moreover, that the fate of countries and kings was more than once determined by the decisions of some assembly of devil-worshippers. At a secret Luciferian sabbat in 1786, for example, Cagliostro, Duchanteau, de Langes and other intriguers were present to decide upon the deaths of Louis XVI of France and Gustavus III of Sweden.

The Templars' "Baphomet was preserved in secret for

nearly five centuries", says one writer, "and ultimately carried by one Isaac Long in 1801 with the skull of the last Grand Master, the unhappy Jacques du Molay, from Paris to Charleston, U.S.A." Here the society of Luciferians recommenced, but the direction of the movement was subsequently transferred to Rome by Adriano Lemmi. Luciferian groups held regular assemblies in various centres, at which Christ was abjured and the devil worshipped with obscene rites. A Satanic chapel discovered in Italy in 1895 was draped in black and red, whilst an image of Satan stood between black candles as the object of worship. Groups of Satanists were found in Helsingfors in 1931 and in London in 1934. Four years later, it was alleged that there were 22 chapels in Paris, where the foul ceremonies were carried out with the utmost indecency. Germany, Spain, America and other countries seem to have been infected with the evil. In almost all centres, the idolatrous and blasphemous worship was followed by debauchery, while, in some cases, the worship itself was conducted in a state of nudity. The devil worship and indecent rites of Alastair Crowley and his confederates in the Isle of Capri revealed the degradation to which human beings, controlled by the devil, can eventually descend.

The activities of Satanists in Paris were suppressed for some time, but reappeared in a room in a quiet café, which was converted into a temple of blasphemous ritual. Writing in *The Advent Witness* in 1938, F. W. Pitt described the scene in this quiet Parisian street: "The worshippers were in the habit of assembling nightly in the café, proceeding to an upstairs room, which had thick doors and iron shutters and was protected from prying eyes with heavy curtains inside. People of all ages and both sexes, well-dressed men and women frequented the place. A password was used. Here the Black Mass was celebrated nightly. There was an altar covered with black, on which was set up an effigy of the devil. The ceremony was a travesty of Christian worship. Some of the women attendants in the congregation were closely veiled and others wore male attire. Fashionable people came in motors, while the chief priest drew up in a carriage drawn by a pair of white horses. In the presence of about 200 people, novices were initiated and the proceedings continued all night." Initiation always involved a repudiation of Christianity and an acknowledgment of the supreme sovereignty of Satan.

It is maintained that similar ceremonies, with all their blasphemy and immorality, are still carried on secretly not only in France but also in Britain. In America, the cult of Satanism, according to one writer, finds many adherents among high school and college students and also "includes many men and women of education, wealth and social position, who practise the immoralities of Sodom and Gomorrah as part of the sacrilegious rites of Lucifer worship. In one place the shrine is in an expensive apartment house and the doorman has no idea of the object of the beautifully gowned women and the handsomely dressed men who alight from their automobiles and travel to the top floor in the elevator. There they convert themselves into semi-savages, discarding all that civilization has given them, and abandoning themselves to orgiastic ritual in worship of the 'cloven-footed one'. The high priestess of the cult, a well-known leader of society, has many well-known disciples, who have sworn themselves to secrecy. Before an altar raised to Satan, the high priestess leads her disciples in reciting allegiance : 'Satan is our master, he is our lord and we are his disciples. O Satan, our master, our lord, we thy disciples worship thee. We pledge ourselves to the performance of every evil thou hast ever conceived, promising to shun every good. We will faithfully follow thy thirteen commandments and will carry out each instruction in the seven books of deadly sins. This we promise, O Satan, our lord!' There is also a blasphemous burlesque of the Last Supper which is too terrible to record." In the last few years, an El Paso woman founded the International Sovereign Order of Devils, the emblem of which is Satan with a pitchfork, and which has as its object the exaltation of Satan.

Satanism is not something which belongs to the past. It has a very grave danger for the present day. In his *Studii Letterari*, the Italian poet Giosue Carducci unwittingly reveals its connection with the old Etruscan paganism and declares that " the hymn to Phoebus Apollo became a hymn to Satan " in his own thinking. In one of his lengthier odes he describes Satan as the god of matter (a reflection of gnosticism) and rejoices in his return. The following brief extracts will indicate the worship he strives to incite for the evil one :

> " To thee my verses, unbridled and daring,
>   Shall mount, O Satan, king of the banquet,
>   Away with thy sprinkling, O priest, and thy droning,
>   For never shall Satan, O priest, stand behind thee.
>
> Thy breath, O Satan, my verses inspires,
>   When from my bosom the gods I defy.
>   Of kings pontifical, of kings inhuman :
>   Thine is the lightning that sets minds to shaking.
>
> O soul that wanderest far from the straight way,
>   Satan is merciful. See Héloisa !
>
> Like the whirlwind spreading its wings,
>   He passes, O people, Satan the great !
>   Hail, of the reason the great Vindicator !
>   Sacred to thee shall rise incense and vows !
>   Thou hast the god of the priest disenthroned."

The attitude of Theosophy to Satan and Satan-worship is extremely significant, if not indeed startling. In *Isis Unveiled*, for example, Madame Blavatsky contends that the devil is not " the manifestation of any evil principle that is evil in itself, but only the shadow of the Light." Anna Kingsford goes even farther when she writes of the evil one, " Among the gods there is none like unto him, into whose hands are committed the kingdoms, the power, and the glory of the world, thrones, empires, the dynasties of kings, the fall of nations, the birth of churches, the triumphs of time." This is nothing less than sheer blasphemy, but Madame Blavatsky declares that, " when the church, therefore, curses Satan, it curses the cosmic reflection of God : it anathematises God made manifest in matter, or in the objective : it maledicts God, or the ever-incomprehensible Wisdom revealing itself as Light and Shadow, good and evil in Nature, in the only manner comprehensible." Here is the modern version of Persian dualism and of the gnostic worship of the devil. This is again confirmed in *The Secret Doctrine*, in which it is stated that " it is Satan who is the god of our planet, and the only god :" and that " he is one with the Logos, the first son, eldest of the gods ". Theosophy thus aligns itself with the Luciferian who would tear Christ from His throne and supplant Him with Satan and who pours adoration at the feet of the great deceiver of mankind.

In his earliest history, proud Lucifer probably sought to

divert the worship of the celestial hosts to himself instead of to his Maker. His desires and purposes are unchanged. He still seeks to seduce men from allegiance to God and to attract their worship to himself. We have here referred to some of the grosser forms of devil-worship: these are only a few of the ways in which the race is drawn aside. Satan's appeal varies with every individual, and where grossness would only repel, the subtler and more insidious course is pursued; but the object remains the same — that homage due only to the Creator may be attracted to the creature.

CHAPTER XIV

THE FUTURE

REINFORCED by the myriads of his spirit hosts, Satan possesses a power which is beyond human comprehension, and which might well give birth to fear in the hearts of men. That power, however, is at present kept in check by a greater authority. "Ye know what restrains," wrote the apostle Paul. "There is He who restrains now until He be gone" (2 Thess. 2: 6, 7). Clearly then there are two hindrances to the full outburst of iniquity — "what restrains" and "He who restrains". There is no difficulty in identifying the latter, for Isaiah says, "when the adversary shall come in like a flood, the Spirit of Jehovah will lift up a standard against him" (Isa. 59: 19). When evil would deluge the world in its overwhelming force, the Holy Spirit effectively holds the torrent in check, and until He is removed, the unhindered manifestation of Satanic power is impossible. But the Holy Spirit at present indwells the individual Christian (1 Cor. 3: 16) and also finds His residence in the church as a whole (Eph. 2: 22), and as long as the Christian and the church are on earth will the Holy Spirit be there also. The presence of God's people is also a preventative of corruption (Matt. 5: 13) and the church could appropriately be described as "what restrains" These hindrances will be removed at Christ's descent to the air to rapture the church from earth to heaven (1 Thess. 4: 15-17; 1 Cor. 15: 51-54), for when the church is caught up, the One who indwells her will be removed at the same time. The devil will then be free to act unrestrainedly, and the lawlessness which is already operating (2 Thess. 2: 7) will culminate in the revelation of "the lawless one" or "Man of Sin" (v. 8).

During the present dispensation, national distinctions have no relevance to the Divine plan. The dispensation is a parenthesis between the 69th and 70th "weeks" of Dan. 9: 25, 26 (see the author's book, *The Climax of the Ages*). During this age the middle wall of partition between Jew and Gentile is broken down (Eph. 2: 14) and God is forming a church, composed of believers in His Son. Not until the complete church has been removed from this earth at the end of this dispensation will the nation of Israel again find a place in His purposes. Already a Jewish State has been established in Palestine, but it is a State in which there is virtually no recognition of God or of His Messiah. The people have returned to their own country, but in unbelief Although the nation is without priest or prophet, the temple will yet be rebuilt in Jerusalem (Matt. 24: 15; 2 Thess. 2: 4) and the Levitical ceremonies reinstituted. The throne is to be filled in a future day by a ruler who is an apostate from his people's ancient faith, and who is prepared to pay divine homage to an even greater ruler (Dan. 11: 36-39). The latter, the supreme sovereign over a western confederacy of ten states (Dan. 7: 7, 8, 23-25), will enter into a seven years' treaty with the Israeli State (the " one week " of Dan. 9: 27), in all probability with the primary object of preserving a buffer state between two other powers, referred to in Dan. 11 as the kings of the north and south (*i.e.* Syria and associated powers in the north and Egypt in the south). The Jewish ruler is described in the Apocalypse as a beast coming up out of the earth (Rev. 13: 11) and " the false prophet " (Rev. 19: 20), while his western associate is described as a beast rising up out of the sea (Rev. 13: 1) and subsequently merely as " the beast " (Rev. 17: 8-13).

Upon " the beast " or western emperor, Satan will bestow his power, throne and authority (Rev. 13: 2), but the real, if invisible, ruler will still be the prince of darkness, and the worshippers of the beast will do homage to the devil who controls him and them. The regal golden fillets are worn, not by the beast, but by the devil (Rev. 12: 3), emphasising that the latter is the actual sovereign. (There are seven heads, or kings, and ten horns, or powers, since in his empire of ten kingdoms the beast will displace three kings and rule over seven subordinates — see Dan. 7: 24; Rev. 17: 12, *etc.*). The great western confederacy will, therefore, be completely dominated by Satan. Nor will Israel be in any more privileged position. The Jewish ruler, " the false prophet ", will speak with the voice of a dragon (Rev. 13: 11), indicating where his allegiance will lie, and his coming is stated to be " according to the working of Satan " (2 Thess. 2: 9).

In Rev. 12, the devil is described as a great red dragon (a type which at once reveals his insatiable voracity and bloodthirsty cruelty), seeking to destroy the Messiah born of Israel and subsequently the godly remnant of Israel who are to suffer the great tribulation. After the ascension of Christ (the Holy Spirit ignores the centuries of the present parenthetical dispensation), the Jewish remnant are depicted as fleeing to a place prepared for their refuge (see also Matt. 24: 16). The apocalyptic seer now saw the outbreak of war in heaven, the angelic forces of Michael the archangel making war upon the hosts of Satan, until ultimately the great adversary was thrust out of heaven and cast down to the earth (Rev. 12: 7-9). His ignominious expulsion was accompanied by a declaration of his true character. He was " the great dragon ", the personification of relentless cruelty; " the ancient serpent ", the subtle deceiver and author of sin; " devil ", the consummate traducer; " Satan ", the unwearying adversary of God's people; and " the accuser of our brethren ", the one who constantly strives to bring the believer into condemnation. Enraged by his fall, Satan will demonstrate his fury to the full during the three and a half years which follow — the period referred to in the Scriptures as that of the great tribulation — and will fill the world with unexampled horrors.

The value of religion in the unification of peoples and nations has been appreciated by many a great ruler of the past and the devil will employ the same practice in his dealings with the western confederacy. The true church will have been raptured from the world, but Satan will introduce his great deception in the form of Babylon the harlot (Rev. 17), a powerful but abominable religious system controlling the State. When the purpose for which the false church has been used, has been achieved, however, the civil authorities will turn and rend Babylon to pieces and plunder it of wealth and possessions. Popular religion will then give way to blatant atheism and rank infidelity until arrested by another event. The presumptuous Antichrist, inspired by the devil, will utter impudent blasphemies against God, concluding by sitting down in the temple of God and claiming divine honours (2 Thess. 2: 4). The Apocalypse reveals that, under his instructions, an image of the beast will be constructed, to which he will give breath and empower it to speak, and that to this image all will be compelled to do homage (Rev. 13: 14, 15). Satanic effort will have achieved world-wide idolatry. Those who refuse to accept Christ will accept the impostor and believe the lie (2 Thess. 2: 11).

Simultaneously with Satan's activities, the wrath of God

will be unleashed and all the judgments of Rev. 6-16 poured out, this poor earth experiencing wars and rumours of wars, famines, pestilences and earthquakes (Matt. 24: 6, 7). At the same time, the activity of evil spirits will be intensified and their numbers increased tremendously (Rev. 9: 1-11).

When human and Satanic wickedness have reached their zenith, the Son of Man will appear in glory, with the hosts of His redeemed behind Him, riding forth to execute judgment upon a guilty world (Zech. 14: 3-5; Jude 14; Rev. 19: 11-16). None will be able to withstand that mighty Conqueror, and the armies of Satan's two puppets, the beast and the false prophet, will be destroyed, whilst the two leaders themselves will be taken and cast alive into the lake of fire — the first inhabitants of that awful place (Rev. 19: 20). Nor will the devil escape. John writes, " I saw an angel descending from heaven, having the key of the abyss, and a great chain in his hand. And he laid hold of the dragon, the ancient serpent, who is the devil and Satan, and bound him a thousand years, and cast him into the abyss, and shut and sealed it over him, that he should not any more deceive the nations until the thousand years were completed " (Rev. 20: 1-3). His plans frustrated, his power broken, and his kingdom temporarily dispelled, the proud Lucifer will suffer ignominious fettering and imprisonment in an unfathomable abyss. In the New Testament, " the abyss " appears to be synonymous with the prison of the evil spirits (see Luke 8: 31). The expression occurs seven times in the Revelation, and always as the abode or prison of evil spirits or demons. " At one time it is closed and locked," writes Jennings. " At another its key is put into the hand of one in whom we discern Satan himself (chap. 9), and he is permitted to allow its inhabitants to return to this earth to add their baleful influence to the evil powers already there. Thus the very latest condition of Gentile government in the finally revived Roman Empire is so revived and energised by those demons, as itself to be said to come ' out of the abyss ' (chap. 11: 7; 17: 8)." For a thousand years Satan will be confined to the sealed prison of the abyss, his power to deceive the world or to seduce the individual temporarily at an end. Nor are his evil emissaries allowed greater freedom than their leader. " In that day Jehovah will punish the host of the high ones, on high, and the kings of the earth upon the earth. And they shall be shut up in prison, and after many days shall they be visited " (Isa. 24: 21, 22). The following verse makes it clear that this will occur when Jehovah reigns in glory on Mount Zion and in Jerusalem. In order that no unworthy influence may intrude, the vast company of the forces of evil will be confined to the abyss for the whole of the millennium: righteousness will reign and peace will be all-pervasive (Isa. 11: 9; 65: 18-25).

During the thousand years' reign of the Messiah, righteousness and equity will be the principles of government, but since human nature is still unchanged, there will be many to whom such principles are repellent. Such will shrink from the infinite holiness of God's earthly centre and in their antipathy to the Messianic rule, will retreat as far from Jerusalem as possible — to use the words of the Apocalypse, " to the four corners of the earth " (Rev. 20: 8). Over the centuries, the number of those who are antagonistic to Divine righteousness and holiness will increase to a considerable extent, until at the close of the millennium, vast numbers will be opposed in heart to their great Benefactor. At that moment, Satan will be released from his prison (Rev. 20: 7). Nothing is said of his angelic forces, but since the subsequent events could scarcely be brought about by the activity solely of one creature, however powerful, it must be assumed that they will be liberated with him. Indeed Isa. 24: 22 explicitly states of the spiritual powers who are imprisoned in the abyss that " after many days shall they be visited ". It is interesting to note that precisely the same words were addressed to Gog in Ezek. 38: 8 and that the Gog and Magog of Ezek. 38 and 39 reappear in Rev. 20: 8 among the supporters of Satan in the last great conflict. While it is possible that the particular nations referred to may still have a history after millennium, it may perhaps be arguable that the Apocalyptic God and Magog are spiritual forces rather than physical ones, but this cannot be propounded dogmatically.

Unchanged in character, Satan's undeviating purpose will still be the frustration of the Divine plans and the overthrow of God's Beloved. He will accordingly seek out the potential rebels, who have gravitated to the remote corners of the earth. The precise nature of his appeal to these rebellious nations is not indicated. The superior position of Israel and the consequent subordination of other nations will have provided sufficient aggravation for the people to be particularly susceptible to the wiles of the devil, and a suggestion that the nations should establish their own government and overthrow that of Messiah would doubtless meet with ready acceptance. With bitter hatred, Satan will therefore organise a last desperate effort to overthrow the Son of God. The complete and incurable depravity of the human heart then becomes manifest. Despite the countless blessings of the millennium, the beneficence of Messiah's rule, and the perfect equity of government, those whom Satan gathers together against Jerusalem will be as numberless as the sand on the seashore. During the thousand years, representatives of all nations will be required annually to attend the Feast of Tabernacles at Jerusalem (Zech. 14: 16) and Govett suggests that the final attack on Jerusalem will take place at the festival time since less suspicion would attach to a large gathering at that time. Inspired by the inveterate and bitter hatred of their invisible leader, the vast armies will set forth to make war on the Lamb and the saints.

Not a weapon will be used in that final conflict. God will intervene before a sword is unsheathed and retributive fire will fall from heaven upon the rebellious masses and utterly consume them (Rev. 20: 9). Satan will now have reached the end of his long career of opposition to his Creator. His power completely shattered, his earthly forces destroyed, and his diabolical plans for ever dissolved, he will hear the dread pronouncement of his eternal and irrevocable doom. Once "the son of the morning" and "the anointed cherub", proud Lucifer will be cast for ever into the lake of fire, to join his two coadjutors, the beast and the false prophet. His angels will find their end similarly in that awful place of suffering, long prepared for them (Matt. 25: 41), and there will he and they "be tormented day and night for ever and ever" (Rev. 20: 10). The present prison of the fallen angels is described as "Tartarus" (2 Pet. 2: 4; Jude 6), although many fallen spirits are or will be detained in "the pit of the abyss" (Luke 8: 31; Rev. 9: 1), but the place of the final doom of Satan and his hosts is named as "Gehenna" (Matt. 25: 41; Rev. 20: 11-15). "No remission is visualised, no relief is intimated. The one who has brought such untold suffering and sorrow to the millions of earth right down the ages, must himself bear the penalty of his folly 'day and night for the ages of the ages'. Human mind fails to grasp the immensity of the expression but the awful tragedy of

Lucifer's fall can only emphasise the grace meted out to the human sinner" (*Prophecy's Last Word*). Well has Chafer written, "the present time is, for Satan, the struggle for his own existence, as well as the realisation of all that has been his ambition in the ages past. The warfare is no mere passing amusement for him, for he, in desperation, is facing a terrible and awful judgment if he cannot succeed in his purpose. The spectacle now presented to all enlightened beings of the universe, is that of a mighty celestial being, the god of this earth, who was by creation the full measure of perfection, both in wisdom and beauty, making his last and most desperate warfare, both to realise his own ambition and to thwart every movement of the Most High: knowing that in failure there is no ground for mercy, but only the terrible destruction that has been so long predicted. He knew when he formed this God-dishonouring purpose that it must either wholly succeed or he himself fall into terrible judgment."

No hope is held out for Satan in the Scriptures. The possibility of his repentance and restoration is sometimes mooted, but it is an entirely unscriptural idea. Giovanni Papini, for example, says, "The Christian . . . should feel for him as the most supremely unfortunate of created beings, the leader and symbol of all enmity and division, yet the archangel who once was nearest to God. Perhaps only our love can help him to save himself, help him become again what he once was, the most perfect of heavenly spirits. If Satan can be freed from the hatred of Christians, men would be forever freed from Satan. . . . Is it not possible that Christ redeemed men so that, following this precept to love their enemies, they may one day be worthy of conceiving the redemption of the most ominous and stubborn enemy of all? . . . We must approach Satan in a spirit of mercy and justice, not in order to become his admirers or imitators but with the hope of freeing him from himself and ourselves thereby from him. Perhaps he awaits only a sign of our mercy to find once again in himself the strength to renounce his hatred, that is, to free the whole world from the dominion of evil." We have quoted at length in order that the danger of this teaching (which is by no means uncommon) may be appreciated. There can be no fraternisation with evil and no sympathy for the evil one. The Word of God shows clearly and without doubt that Satan's final end is eternal banishment from God.

Faced with such a mighty antagonist, the children of God need daily to draw upon the grace and strength which is placed at their disposal. The revelation given in the Scriptures of the power of the great opponent of the truth surely inspires the heart with praise and gratitude for the wonderful deliverance which has been wrought by the Son of God, but at the same time, emphasises the need for complete dependence upon Him, in Whom is all strength. The susceptibility of the flesh and the subtlety of the devil combine to weaken the defence, but the believer wars not at his own charges. All the resources and rich treasures of God — His strength, His power, His might — are accessible to the child of God through Christ, and are appropriated by faith through prayer. Schweitzer connects this interestingly with the Lord's Prayer. He says, "In the Lord's Prayer, He makes believers to pray to God that God will not lead them into the afflictions brought about by the powers of evil . . . but will deliver them forthwith from the power of the 'Wicked One' (Matt. 6: 13). God does not remain passive in all this, however, for 'the angel of Jehovah encampeth round about them that fear Him, and delivereth them' (Psalm 34: 7). Greater is He that is for us than he that is against us."